SECRET CHRISTCHURCH

Andrew Jackson

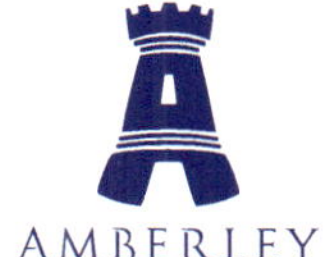

AMBERLEY

First published 2024

Amberley Publishing
The Hill, Stroud
Gloucestershire, GL5 4EP

www.amberley-books.com

ISBN 978 1 3981 2155 3 (print)
ISBN 978 1 3981 2156 0 (ebook)

British Library Cataloguing in Publication Data.
A catalogue record for this book is available from the
British Library.

Origination by Amberley Publishing.
Printed in Great Britain.

Contents

Introduction

During the Neolithic period (9000–3000 BC) through to the Bronze Age (3000–1200 BC), to the Iron Age (1200–600 BC) and the Roman invasion (AD 43), England consisted of numerous disparate indigenous Celtic tribes, including the powerful Durotriges, who lived in what is now Dorset, South Wiltshire, South Somerset and East Devon.

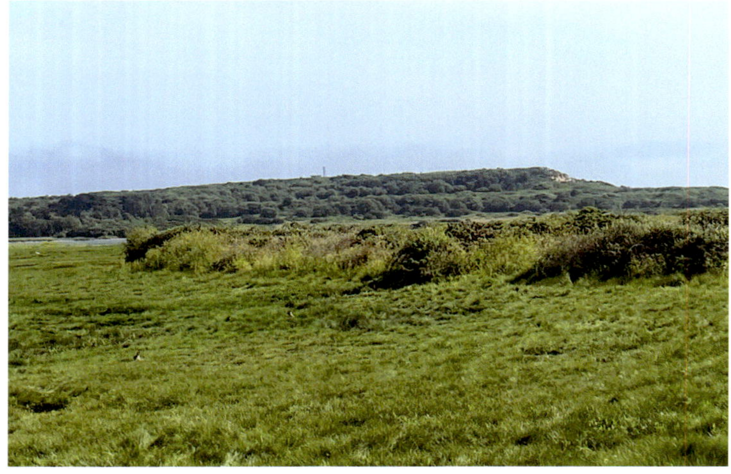

Hengistbury Head.

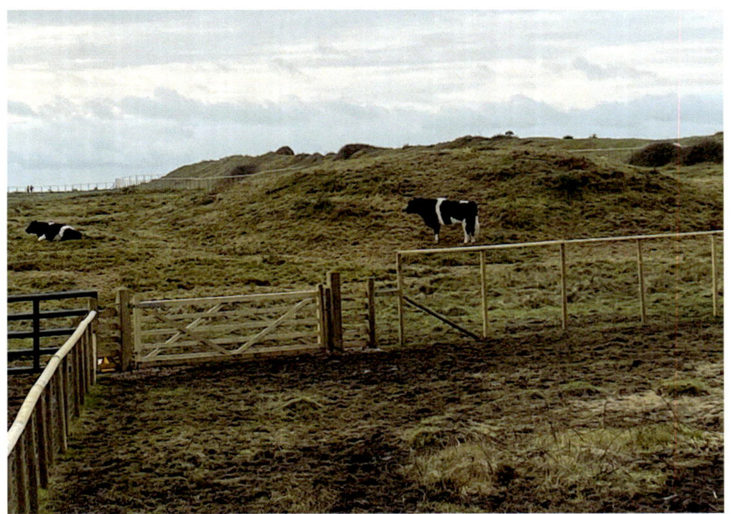

This barrow near the Hengistbury Head Visitor Centre is one of ten large barrows on the headland which are thought to be ancient burial mounds. The artifacts found within this barrow have led archaeologists to believe that a woman of high status was buried here.

It is believed that from the end of the Neolithic period to the beginning of the Bronze Age that the Durotriges made use of Hengistbury Head as a place of burial, ritual and ceremony. Later, during the Iron Age they recognised that the land was endowed with a good supply of iron ore, so began to actually settle on the headland from around 700 BC. During this period, cross-channel trading links were also established, meaning that Christchurch can claim to be England's oldest port. Furthermore, Hengistbury Head marked the coastal end point of a series of Dorset Iron Age forts, the others in the chain being Hambledon Hill, Hod Hill, Maiden Castle, Spetisbury Rings, Badbury Rings and Dudsbury Camp.

The harbour was surrounded by the marshy land around the Stour and Avon rivers, so provided a safe anchorage. The area was also well fortified by two ditches or double dykes which separated the headland from the mainland and were constructed in a similar way to those the Durotriges had also built at their main base of Maiden Castle, Dorchester.

Prior to the Roman invasion of Britain in AD 43, the harbour prospered as one of the most important route-ways in Britain. Then as the Roman Empire expanded its boundaries northwards, exotic goods began to arrive from Italy, France and the Channel Islands, which in turn were traded for goods from southern England.

After the Roman invasion, Hengistbury Head continued to thrive as the Romans created other larger ports along the south coast, while the Durotriges, and then later a Romano British community, continued to live on the headland until around AD 350.

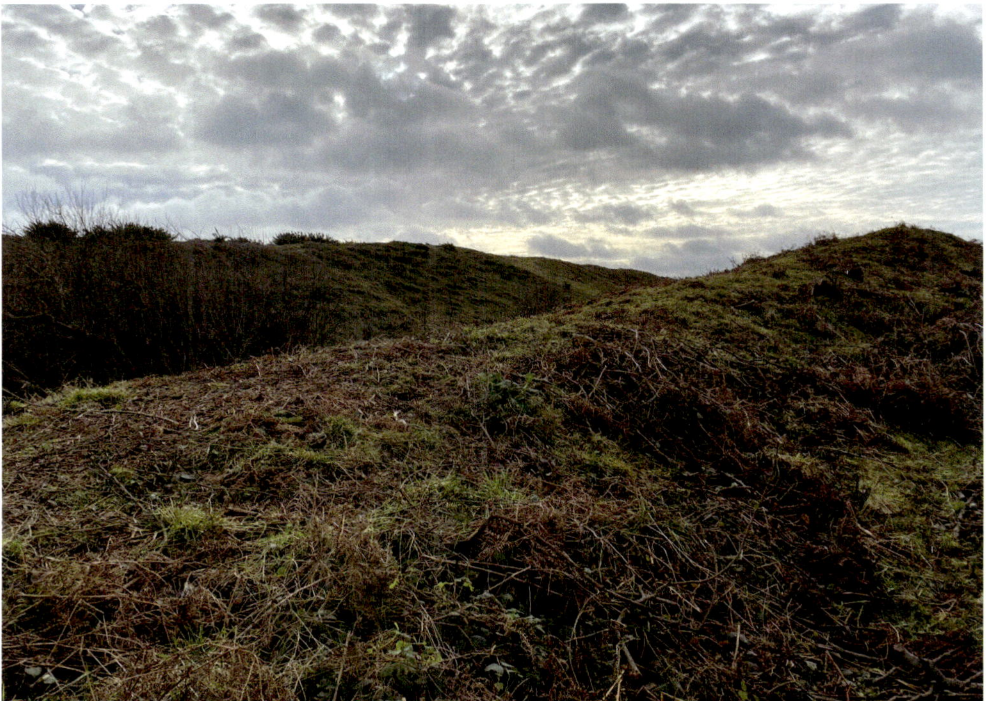

The Hengistbury Head Double Dykes – they were considerably larger during the Iron Age.

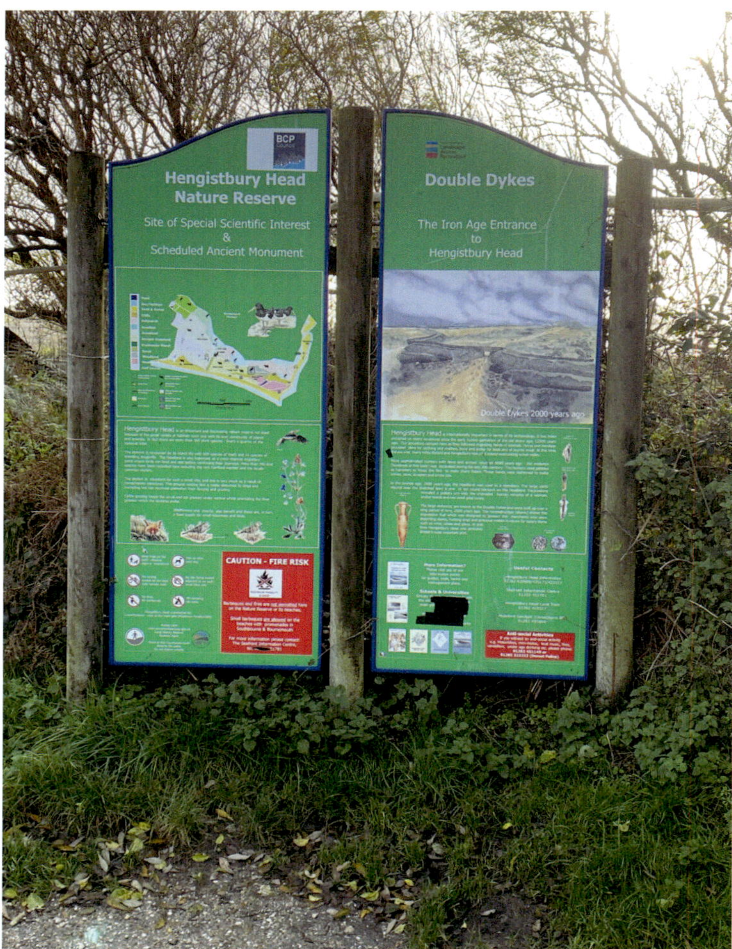

The Double
Dykes sign,
Hengistbury Head.

Later, Alfred the Great (r. 871–899), King of the West Saxons (Wessex), realised the need to consolidate his kingdom in order to effectively defend it against the frequent forays of the Viking raiders. Accordingly, he established a programme of building fortified settlements known as burghs, which resulted in Wessex being the only Anglo-Saxon kingdom to successfully repel the Danish Viking invasions of the ninth century. The Burgh of Twyneham (the Anglo-Saxon name for Christchurch) then went on to become one of the most important fortifications on the south coast due to its sheltered harbour and strategic defensive position.

Did You Know?
Twyneham meant the confluence of two rivers in Anglo-Saxon dialect/language.

Twyneham developed into an important religious centre when a Saxon church was founded in 1043 by Edward the Confessor (r. 1042–1066). However, after the arrival of the Normans, King William II (r. 1087–1100), made Ranulf Flambard, who was the most ruthless, powerful and feared baron in England, Dean of Twyneham. The ambitious Flambard then sought to increase the prestige of the town and in 1094 instigated the building of a larger, more imposing church at St Catherine's Hill, a mile away from the site of the original Saxon church.

Legend has it that the builders were beset by problems of materials going missing overnight, only for them to turn up at the site of the original church the following morning. It seemed that God, moving in mysterious ways, was indicating that the site should be at the original church. A further indication came when construction was eventually moved to the original site, and an extracurricular carpenter, who wasn't on the payroll, joined the workers.

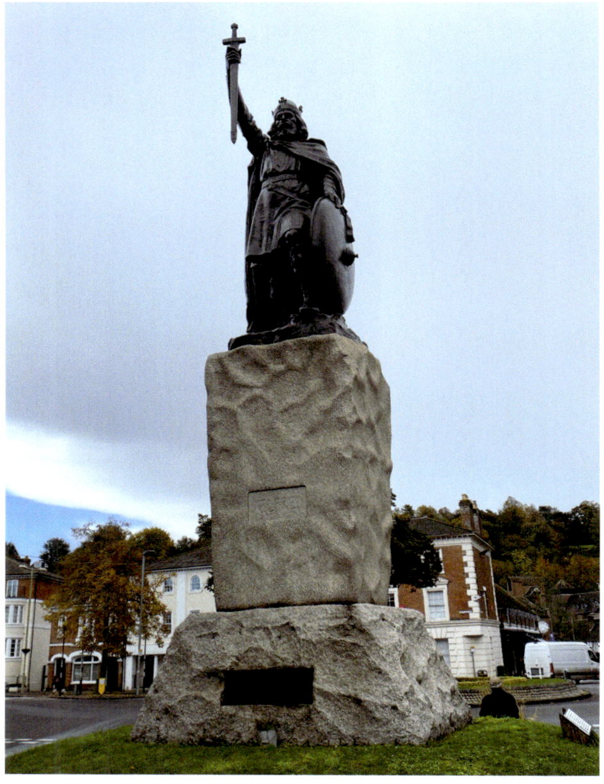

King Alfred's statue at Winchester.

One day a huge wooden beam was cut too short, and therefore wouldn't fit into its intended position. However, the following day, the beam was miraculously the correct size, and had been slotted into place. The enigmatic tradesman had also disappeared, confirming the builders' suspicions that the mystery man must have been a certain well-known carpenter from Nazareth.

This story spread far and near, and the church became known as Christ's Church, which led eventually to the town also being called Christchurch and becoming a place of pilgrimage, which in turn, much to Flambard's delight, further enhanced the status of the town.

In 1100, King William II, known as Rufus due to his red hair, was killed in suspicious circumstances – apparently by the knight Walter Tyrrell, whilst hunting not far from Christchurch in the New Forest. However, Rufus' brother, who was among the hunting party, also aroused much suspicion, as he galloped away from the scene and seized the treasury at Winchester Castle and then with indecent haste was crowned at Westminster Abbey as King Henry I (r. 1100–1135).

Henry wasted no time in sending Flambard to the Tower of London and instead awarded his most loyal and trusted advisor, the baron Richard de Redvers, with numerous estates, including the manor and borough of Christchurch. During this period, the defences of the castle were expanded and improved and a thriving market town began to emerge in the shadow of the castle and priory, which also went hand in hand with the development of the harbour as a fishing port.

Christchurch backed the Royalist cause during the English Civil War (1642–1651), but the town and castle were captured by Parliamentary troops in 1644. The Royalist's made several attempts to regain the town, but it remained in Parliamentary hands until the end of the conflict.

In the seventeenth and eighteenth centuries, fishing and boat building were the prime economies; although for others, the sheltered harbour and marshland adjacent to the two rivers provided ideal opportunities for the black economy occupation of smuggling. By the early nineteenth century, 'the trade' as it was euphemistically known had become an illicit additional income for many, but for others, such as certain notorious gang leaders, it provided a lot more than a supplementary income and was a major source of wealth.

King George III (r. 1760–1820) frequently visited the town in order to indulge in the new-fangled hobby of sea bathing and in so doing established Christchurch as a suitable seaside resort for the aristocracy. However, later after the 'coming of the railway' in 1847, the hoi polloi also started to arrive to enjoy the sun, sea and sand.

During the Second World War, Christchurch braced itself for an anticipated possible invasion and the town was fortified with pill boxes, gun emplacements and tank traps, while the beaches were covered with barbed wire and mines. The town also became a centre of aircraft manufacture and played a significant role in helping to put Britain at the forefront of world aviation between the 1940s and 1970s.

After the war, Christchurch continued as a small market town until the middle of the twentieth century, when it started to also become one of the country's most favoured destinations for retirees, which along with Poole and Bournemouth now forms a sprawling conurbation of 465,000 people.

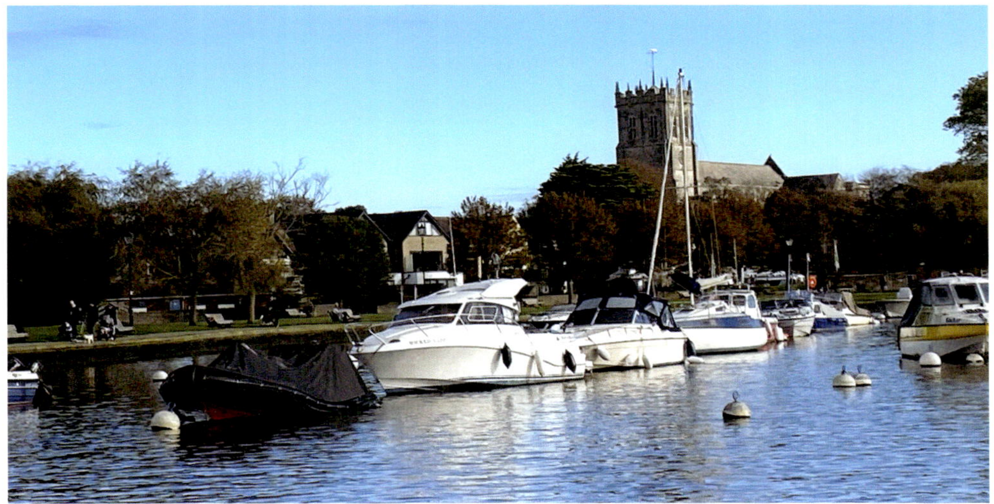

The kind of tranquil scene that makes Christchurch an attractive place to live or visit.

Did You Know?
Christchurch was originally in Hampshire, but boundary changes in 1974 saw it become part of Dorset. The original County Gate roundabout at Westbourne, Bournemouth, used to mark the border between Dorset and Hampshire, but now it signifies the boundary between Poole and Bournemouth.

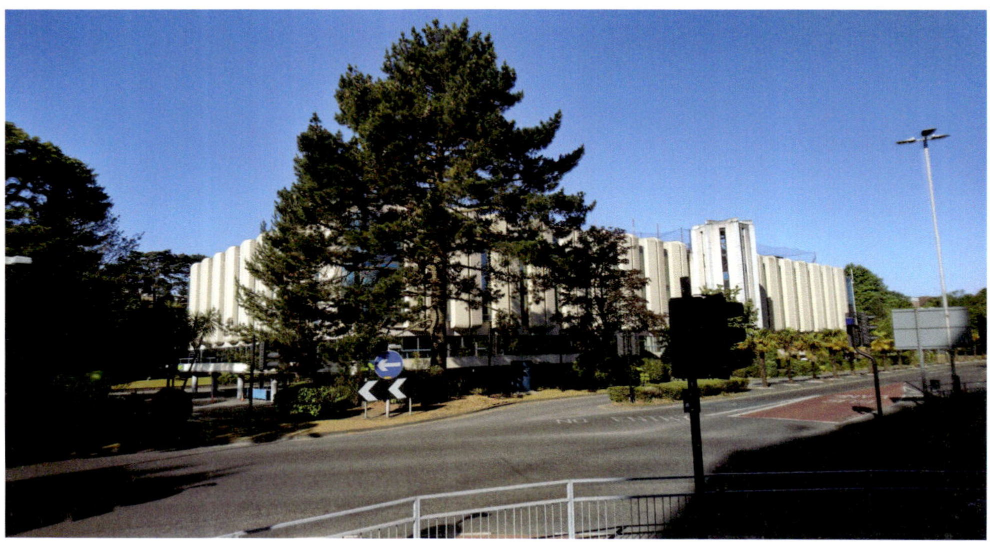

County Gates roundabout.

1. Christchurch's Medieval Connection

The Norman dynasty formed the first part of the medieval period and refers to the time when William I (r. 1066–1087), William II (r. 1087–1100) and Henry I (r. 1100–1135) ruled England. These three monarchs left a lasting impression, as during their incumbencies they secured the borders and brought organisation to government. They also had a major impact on the church and architecture.

Before the Norman Conquest of 1066, a monastery and associated early Christian church existed within the Saxon burgh (*see* Introduction) of Twynham and according to the Domesday Book survey of 1086, twenty-four canons were involved at this site. The strategic location of the burgh at the confluence of the Stour and Avon estuaries afforded the defence of water on three sides, as well as providing an important transport infrastructure and trading access. Nevertheless, when William the Conqueror (William I) came to power, he improved on the basic defensive capabilities of the burgh by strengthening the original fort that had been built by Aethelwold in 901.

Upon William I's death in 1087, his three sons, Robert, William Rufus and Henry, were at loggerheads as they jockeyed for the throne. William I's will granted the crown to William Rufus, rather than to his older son, Robert, who instead had to make do with the Duchy of Normandy. Meanwhile the younger brother, Henry, was left landless, much to his chagrin.

William II (Rufus) was not a religious man and he quickly made an enemy of the all-powerful church, whose wealth he frequently extracted in order to pay for his own grandiose schemes or to simply distribute among his friends. Then in 1089, when Lanfranc, the Archbishop of Canterbury, died, he refused to appoint a replacement for three years, which enabled him to appropriate even more church money for himself. When Lanfranc's successor was eventually appointed, the new man Anselm frequently challenged the monarch, and as a result, was sent into exile. Rufus then adopted the same tactic of delaying the appointment of his successor, in order to continue to plunder the church's wealth.

Rufus also had his work cut out subduing his enemies. He forced the Scottish king to pay homage to him and then violently pacified South Wales. He was also in constant disagreement with his brother Robert, who was not happy that, he as the eldest son had only been given Normandy and had been overlooked for the crown of England. This quarrel was only resolved when Robert joined the First Crusade, with the aid of money lent to him by Rufus.

History records that Rufus kept the unruly barons in order, but was very cruel and vindictive to the common people. However, this interpretation may have been due to the fact that in those times, history was recorded by church scholars, and of course, as he was in dispute with the church throughout his reign, they may not have chronicled his legacy too kindly. However, one aspect of his legacy that was positive (depending how you look at it) was the completion of his pet projects: the Palace of Westminster and Westminster Hall, better known as the Houses of Parliament.

In 1094, King William Rufus made Ranulf Flambard, who was the most powerful, ruthless and feared baron in England, Dean of Twyneham. Flambard had previously held the eminent position of the Keeper of the Seal during the reign of William I and in addition, William II (Rufus) also appointed him Royal Chaplain, Chief Advisor and for a time Chief Justice.

Christchurch continued to be an important religious centre, and to reflect this at the instigation of Flambard, the Normans set about building a large and imposing church at St Catherine's Hill, to replace the existing Saxon church which had been founded in 1043 by Edward the Confessor (r. 1042–1066). A sequence of events (*see* Introduction) then took place resulting in the legend of the Miraculous Beam and the name of the town changing to Christchurch. The town also became a place of pilgrimage, which further enhanced its religious status, leading to further growth.

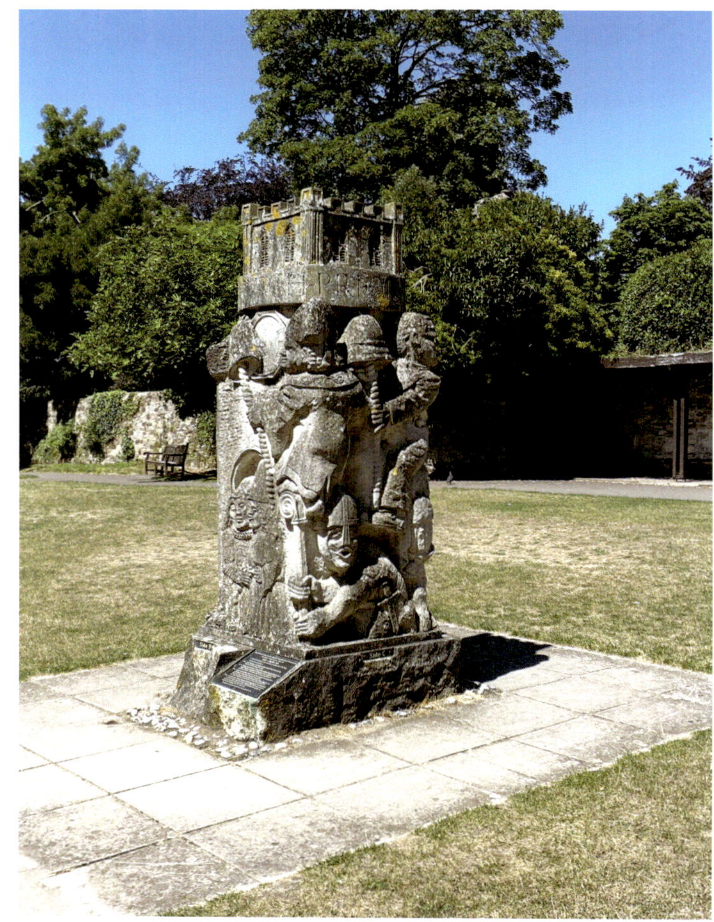

This sculpture was designed by Jonathan Sells, who won a competition to produce a design to be sculpted from Portland stone, to celebrate the 900th anniversary of Christchurch Priory. It depicts events and life at the priory and includes:

1.) Monks studying and working in the priory.
2.) Ranulf Flambard planning the building of the priory in 1094 and later becoming the Bishop of Durham.
3.) The commencement of building of the priory during the Norman period.
4.) The dissolution of the monastic priory in 1539, since when it has served as the parish church.

Flambard was complicit in the king's ruthless extortion of the church and to add insult to injury, he was then given the prestigious church office of Bishop of Durham in 1099. He was deeply unpopular with the common people, as were the numerous mercenary Norman knights who frequented William's court and who often brutally ransacked villages and wrought savage reprisals for minor indiscretions. For instance, the Normans guarded their game with extraordinary ferocity and a poacher was liable to be punished by death for killing a deer, have his hands cut off for shooting at one and be blinded for disturbing one.

Did You Know?
The New Forest is in fact a bit of a misnomer in that it was only actually new in the time of William the Conqueror in 1079, when as in the creation of other royal forests, land was cleared of Saxon villages and reserved as a royal hunting ground. The word forest has come to mean a densely wooded area, but originally it meant simply an area set aside for royal hunting. By the end of the twelfth century one third of England had been claimed as royal forest and the New Forest was one of the earliest. Deer and wild boar were set aside for the king's sport alone, but his barons were allowed to hunt lesser game such as hare and fox.

One of the mercenary knights who was an integral part of William II's extravagant court and who quickly became close to the king was Walter Tyrrell. He was born in Tonbridge, Kent, but according to the Domesday Book was Lord of Poix de Picardie in northern France. He was known to be an excellent bowman and an avid huntsman and as such, he regularly accompanied William Rufus to their favourite hunting ground of the New Forest.

On 1 August 1100, a hunting party including, among many others, King William Rufus, Walter Tyrrell and Prince Henry, spent the night at Malwood Hall near Minstead in the New Forest, where they had a banquet in advance of pursuing the hunt the next day.

After the banquet, Rufus is said to have had a night filled with dreams of ill portent. It has also been said that various monks and old hags had approached him during the day, leading up to the banquet, warning him against the hunting expedition. It is also believed that Tyrrell and Rufus quarrelled that night and that Rufus, who had initially poured scorn on the dreams and warnings, was still sufficiently disturbed to postpone the hunt until the afternoon.

As the hunt commenced, the party spread out as they chased their quarry and according to most accounts William and Tyrrell soon became separated from the others as they went in pursuit of a stag.

No one really knows what happened next apart from the inescapable fact that the king ended up dead, having been shot with an arrow.

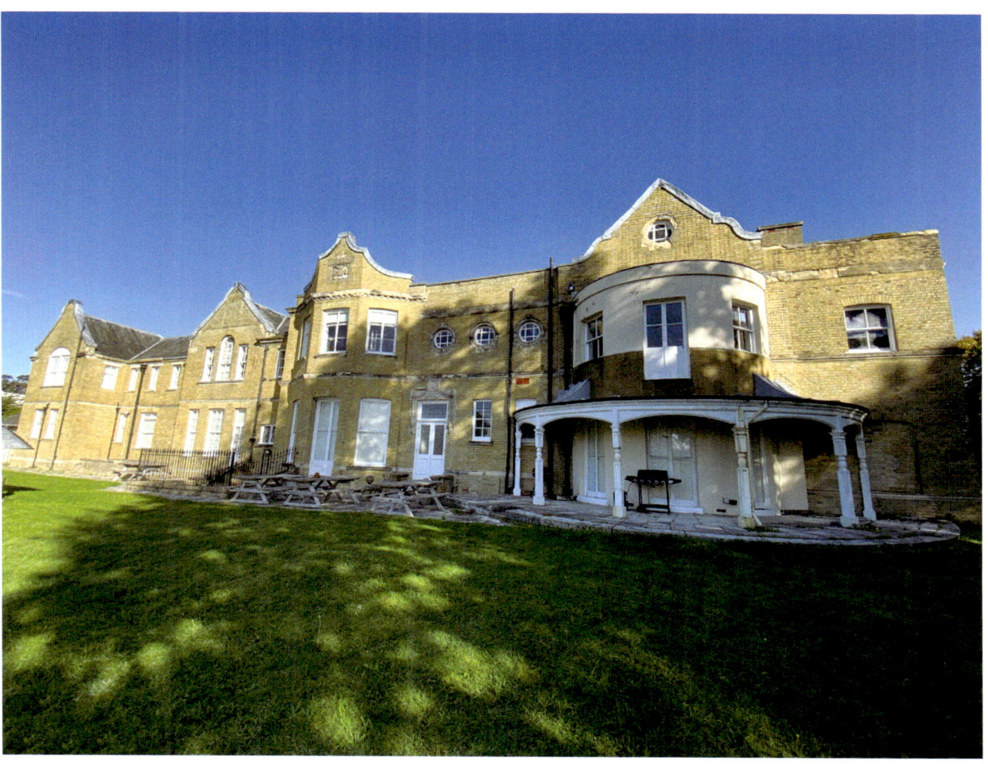

Castle Malwood – which is at the site of what was formerly Malwood Hall, where King Rufus and his hunting party had a banquet before the next day's hunt. It is now a beautiful period property, built sometime between 1802 and 1840, as the property of Colonel Thomas William Robbins, who was wounded at the Battle of Waterloo.

The account given on the Rufus Stone memorial near Minstead in the New Forest is thus:

> The Rufus Stone near Minstead was erected by Earl De La Warr in 1745 and marks the presumed spot where William II was killed by an arrow fired by Walter Tyrrell, while hunting on August 2 1100.
>
> Here stood the oak on which an arrow shot by Sir Walter Tyrrell at a stag glanced and struck King William the second surnamed Rufus on the breast of which he instantly died on 2nd August 1100.
>
> Rufus was laid in a cart belonging to one Purkiss and drawn from hence to Winchester and buried in the cathedral church.

As the king lay dead, Tyrrell mounted his horse and made a swift exit from the scene. Meanwhile it was left to a handful of local peasants to eventually take the body in a cart to be interred at Winchester Cathedral, where the clergy, with whom Rufus had been constantly arguing, refused to perform any religious rites over it.

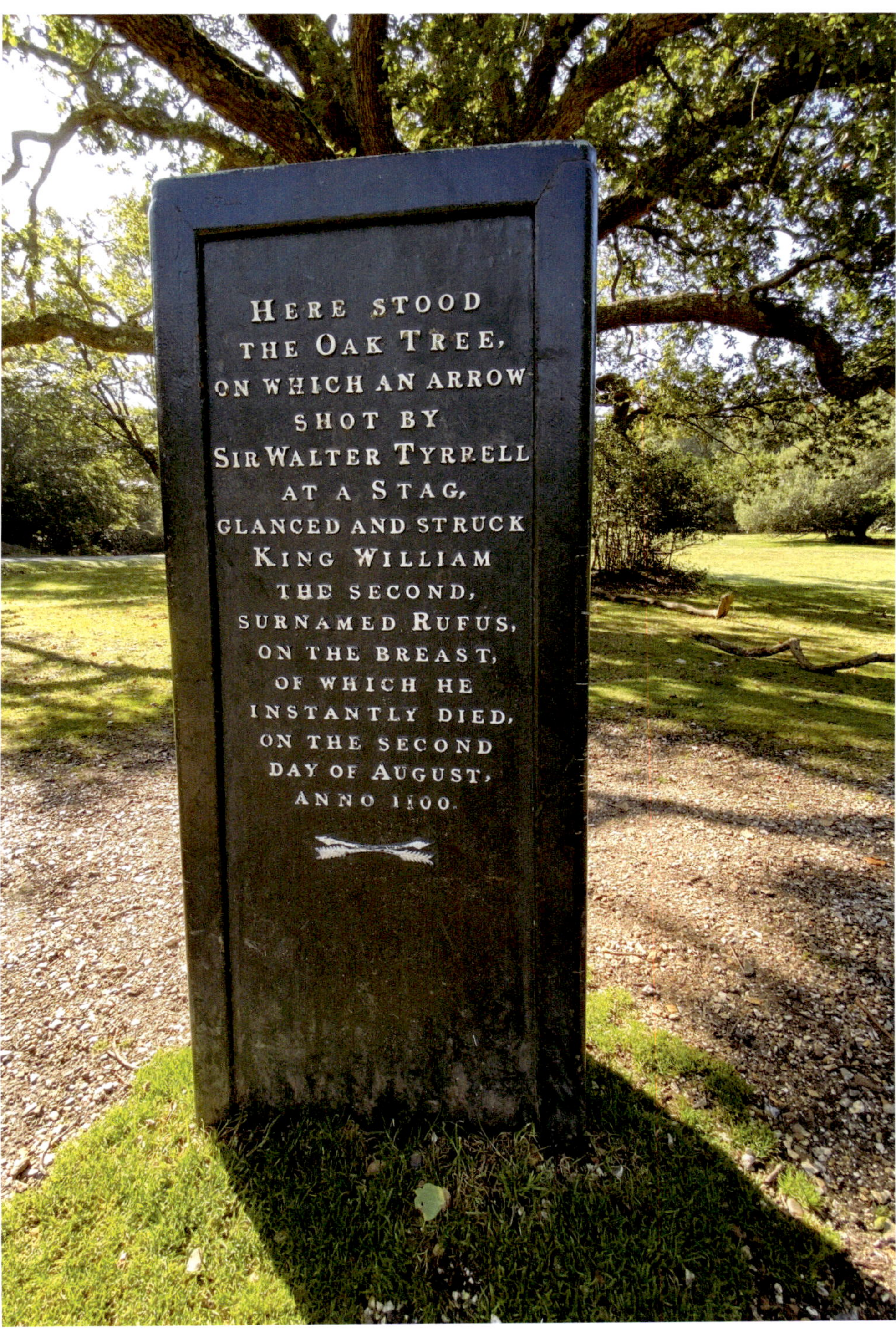

The Rufus Stone.

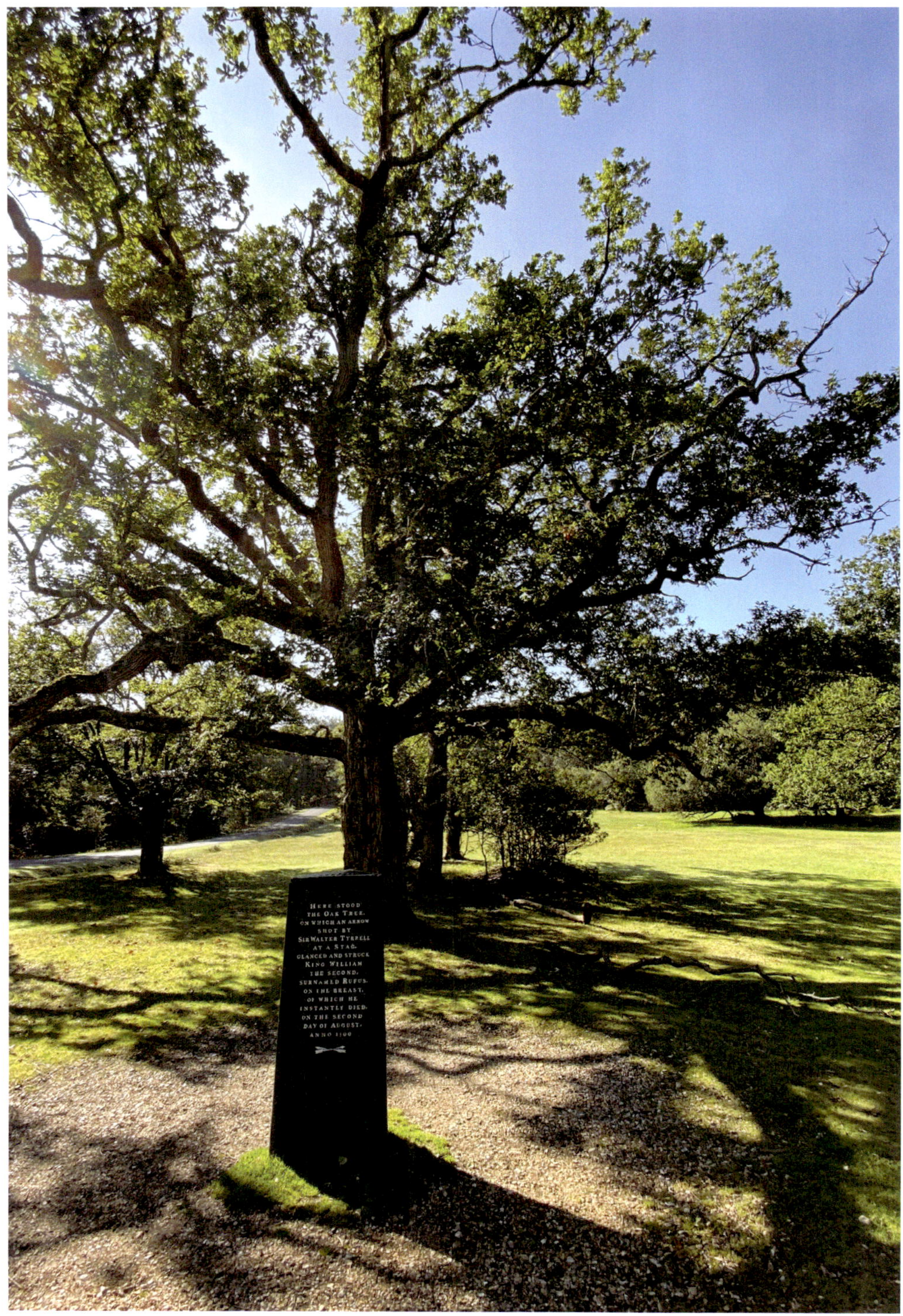

The Rufus Stone and Oak Tree.

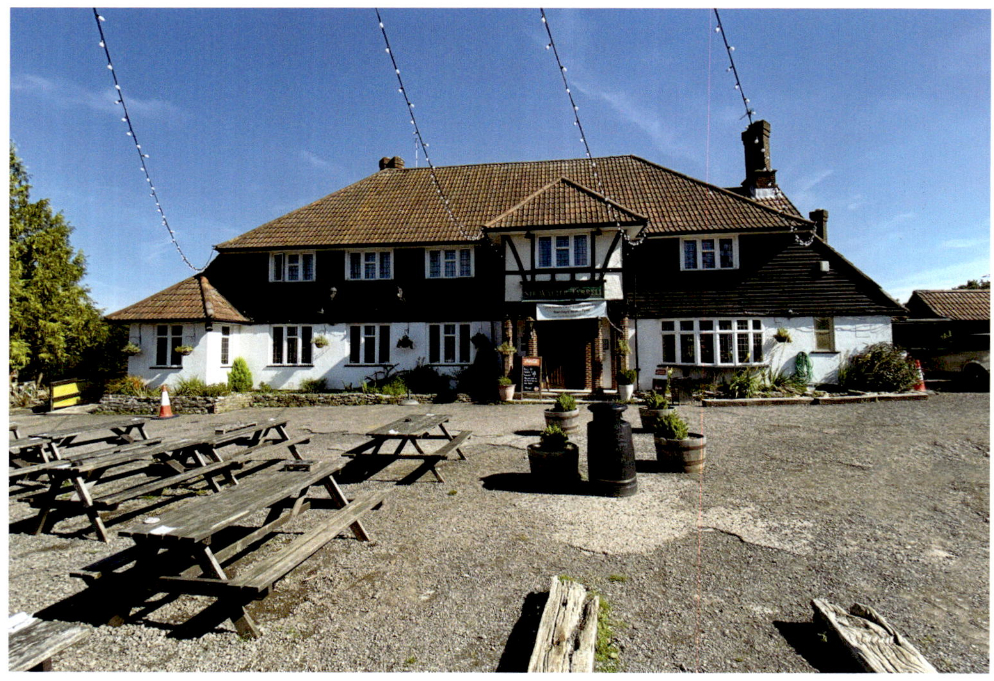

Sir Walter Tyrrell pub.

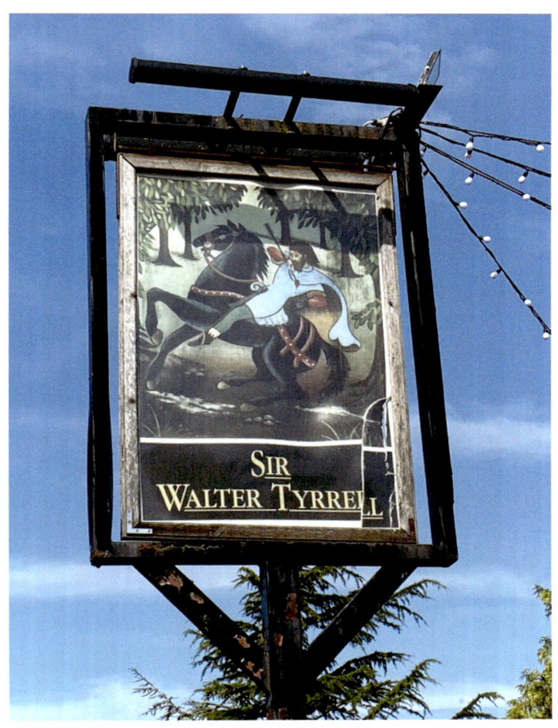

Sir Walter Tyrrell pub sign.

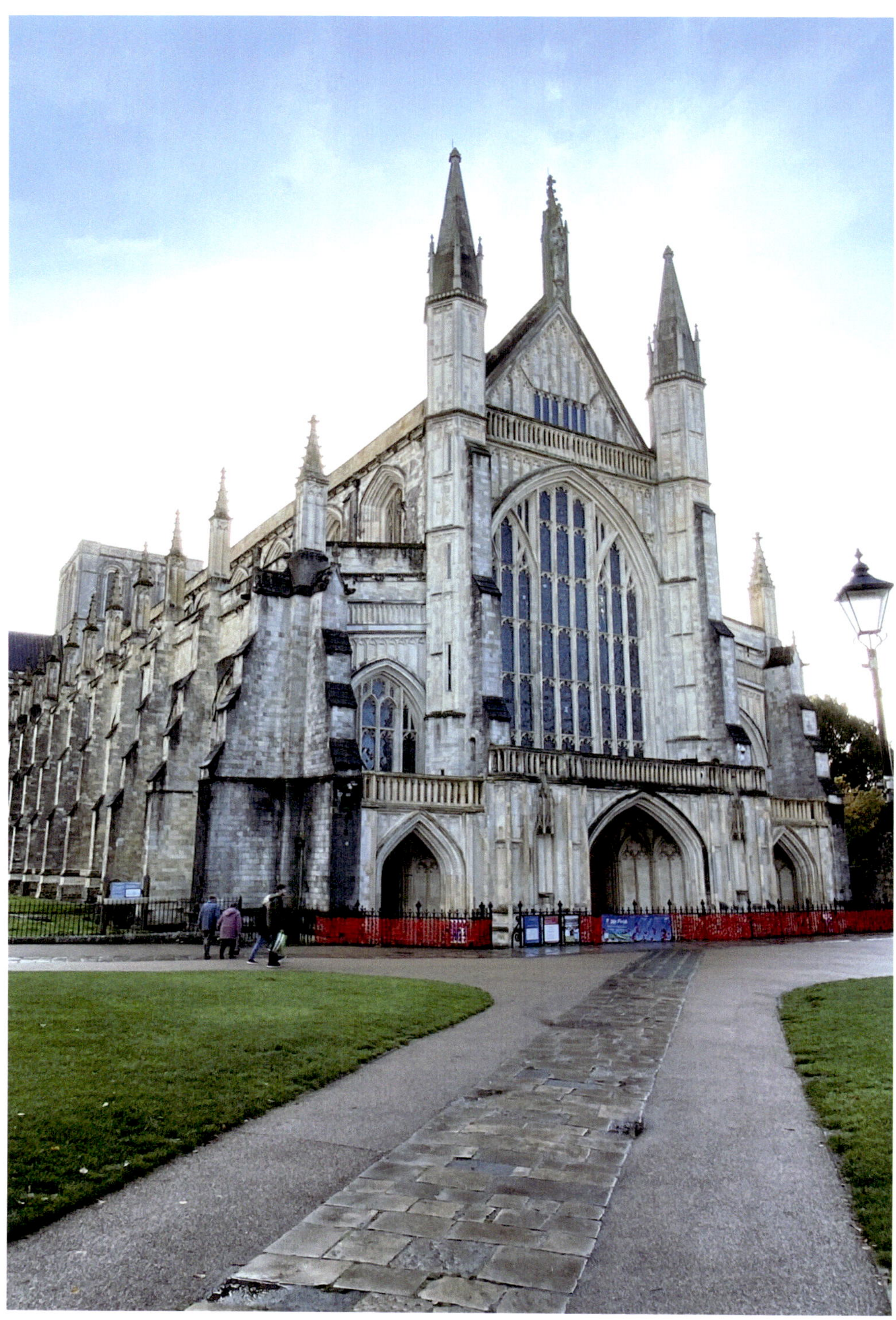

Winchester Cathedral.

King William II (Rufus) was said to have initially been buried under the Great Tower at what was then called the New Minster, before it became Winchester Cathedral. He was not deemed by the church to be suitable to be buried actually within the holy place, which in some ways was a shame as he was the last king to be buried at the cathedral.

However, the Great Tower collapsed in 1107, which was considered by the church to be God's way of showing his disapproval of Rufus. It was rebuilt later in the twelfth century and his remains were removed and placed in one of the mortuary chests that now sit on the screens in the presbytery of the cathedral and contain in addition to William II (Rufus), the remains of Saxon kings, as well as eminent early bishops.

Unfortunately, Cromwell's Parliamentary soldiers severely damaged the mortuary chests in 1642, during the First English Civil War. They totally destroyed six of them and the other four had their contents tipped out. The church officials replaced the bones in the chests as best they could, but to this day, no one knows if the correct bones are in the correct chests – so King William II's bones have now literally joined those of his royal predecessors.

Meanwhile, back in the forest, Sir Walter Tyrrell continued to make good his escape and forded the River Avon near the village of Avon in an area just outside Christchurch which is consequently known as Avon Tyrrell and is close to where the pub the New Queen now stands on the Ringwood Road.

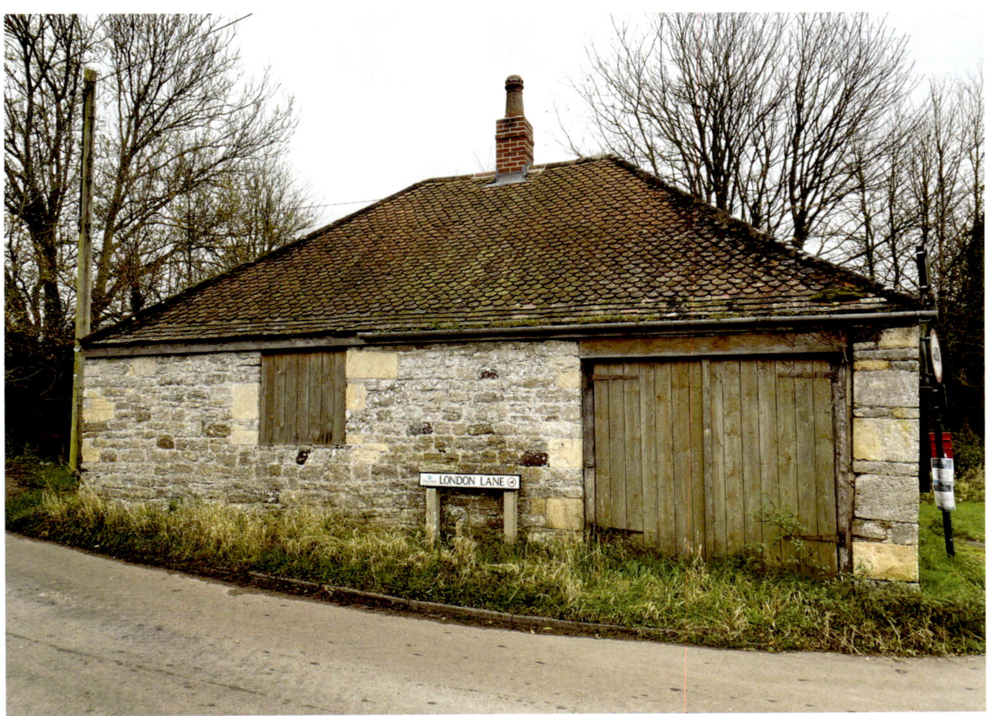

The site of a former blacksmiths on the corner of London Lane, Avon. It is said that Walter Tyrrell had his horse reshod at a blacksmiths in the village of Avon.

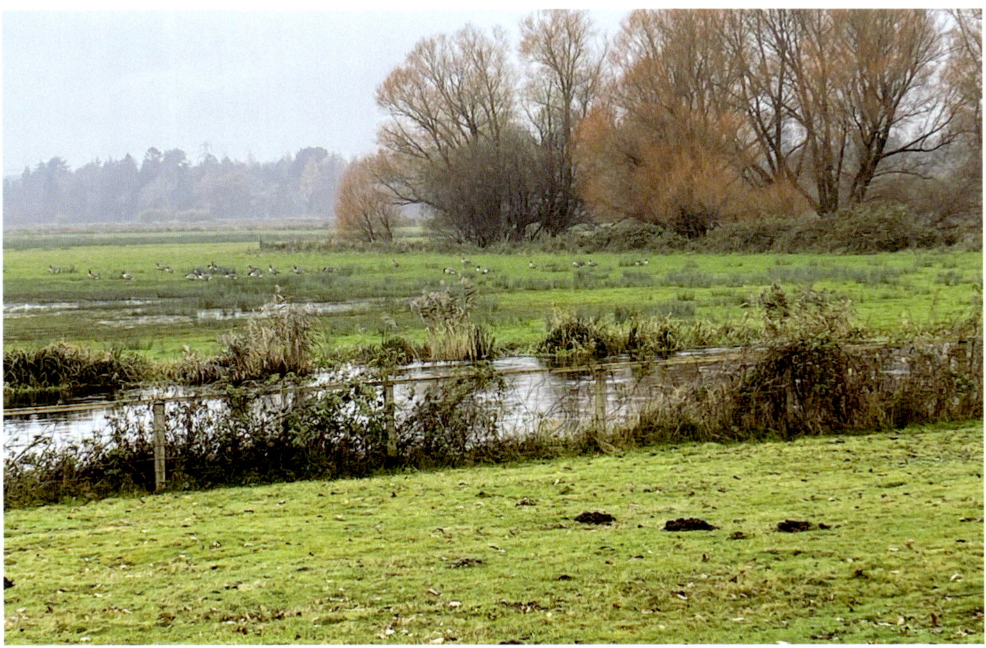

It is thought that Sir Walter Tyrrell crossed the Avon here, whilst making his escape to France via Poole. As a result the area is known as Avon Tyrrell.

Tyrrell made it to Poole from where he successfully escaped to France. No action was ever taken against him and his lands in England were not confiscated. Indeed, his brother-in-law who was also among the hunting party went on to benefit greatly under the new king.

There are several references to Tyrrell's Ford and Walter Tyrrell in this area of Avon Tyrrell.

Did You Know?
A branch of the famous Tyrrell family also emigrated to Australia and are associated with the prestigious Tyrrell's Winery in the Hunter Valley. They even produce a wine called Tyrrell's Rufus Stone.

Prince Henry, William Rufus' younger brother, also hot-footed it from the scene. He abandoned any pursuit of the prime suspect, Tyrrell's and also abandoned the corpse, in order to gallop straight to Winchester Castle where he took the opportunity whilst his older brother, Robert, was away on the Crusades, to hastily seize the treasury. He also had the barons proclaim him as the new king, before heading for London where he was crowned at Westminster Abbey, three days later.

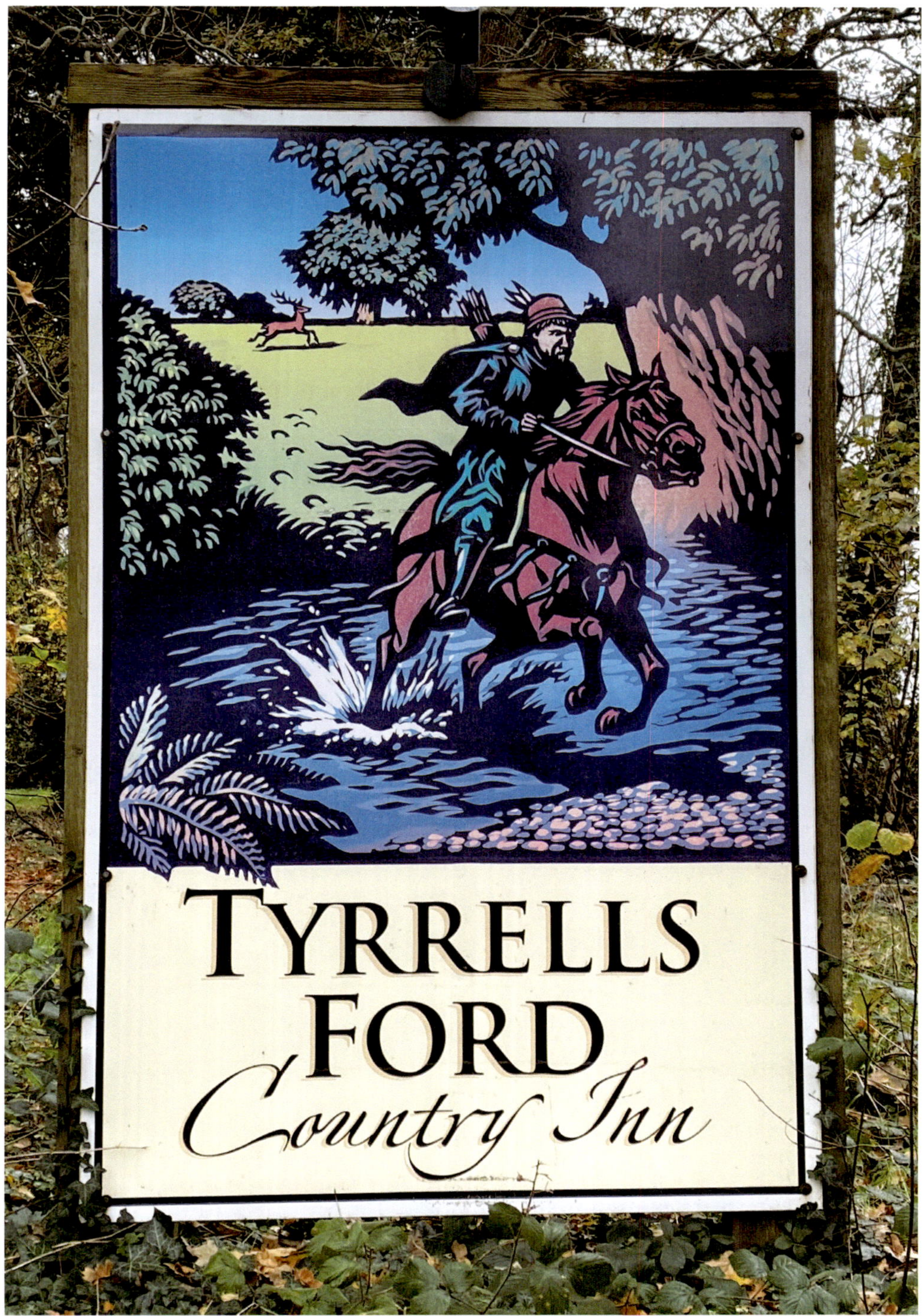

Tyrrells Ford Country Inn and Hotel, an eighteenth-century manor house which was converted to a hotel in the 1970s.

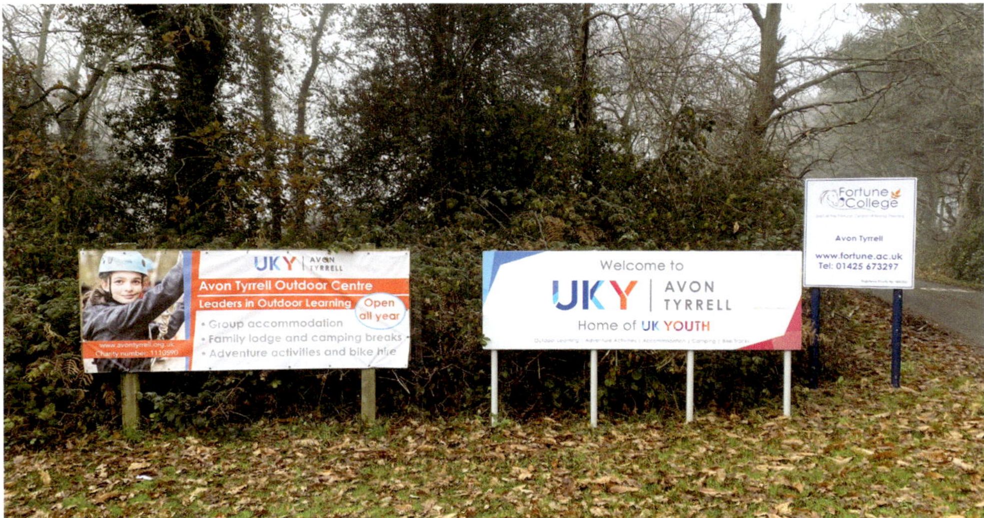

In Norman times the manor of Avon was held by the Peveril family, who held it until 1636, when Sir Thomas Peveril granted the manors of both Avon and Milton to Thomas Tyrrell and subsequently the manor descended in the Tyrrell family, then in later years the Manners family married into the estate and in the 1890s Lord Manners built the now Grade I listed building Avon Tyrrell House, which is now Avon Tyrrell Outdoor Activity Centre.

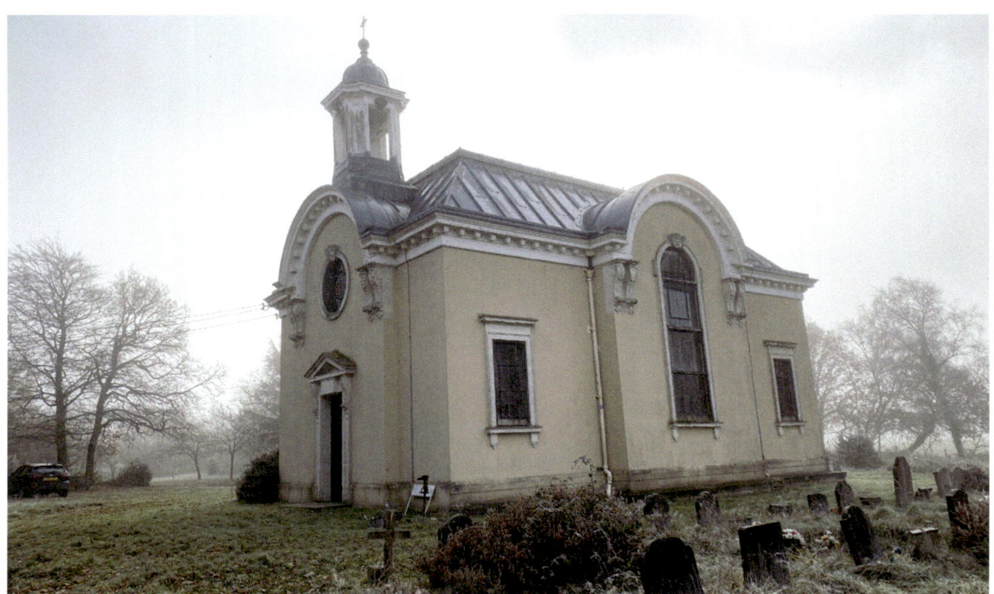

The Avon Tyrrell Estate is a privately owned working arable estate which includes private commercial buildings and private cottages to rent. All Saints Church, Thorney Hill, within the estate was built in 1906 by the Manners family, who currently own the estate. It was built by the third Lord Manners as a memorial to his daughter, who died age seventeen of a fever in India. As well as being a memorial the church also serves as a place of worship for the hamlet of Thorney Hill.

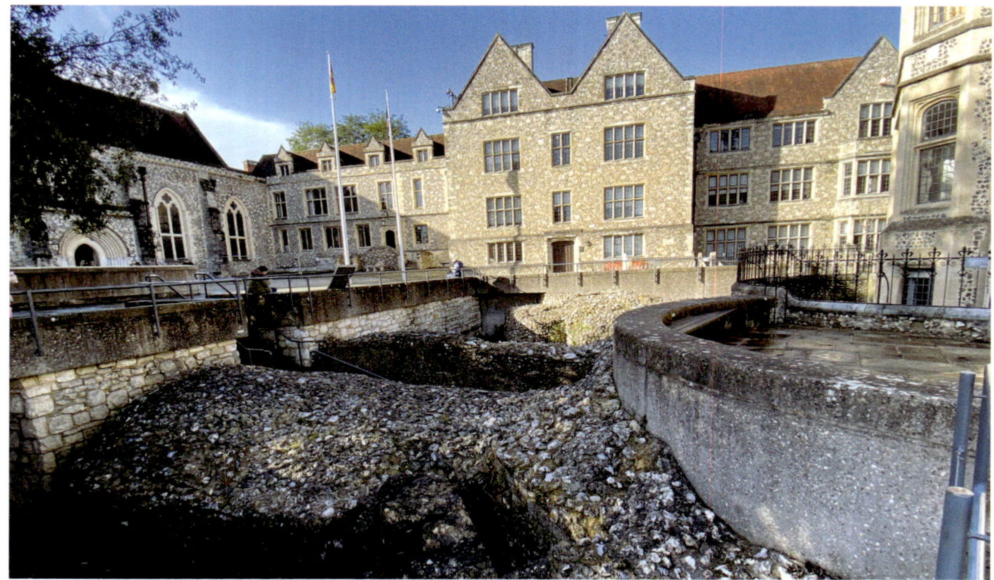

Winchester Castle was founded in 1067 by William the Conqueror and became the centre of Anglo-Norman government, meaning that both the treasury and the exchequer were based at the castle.

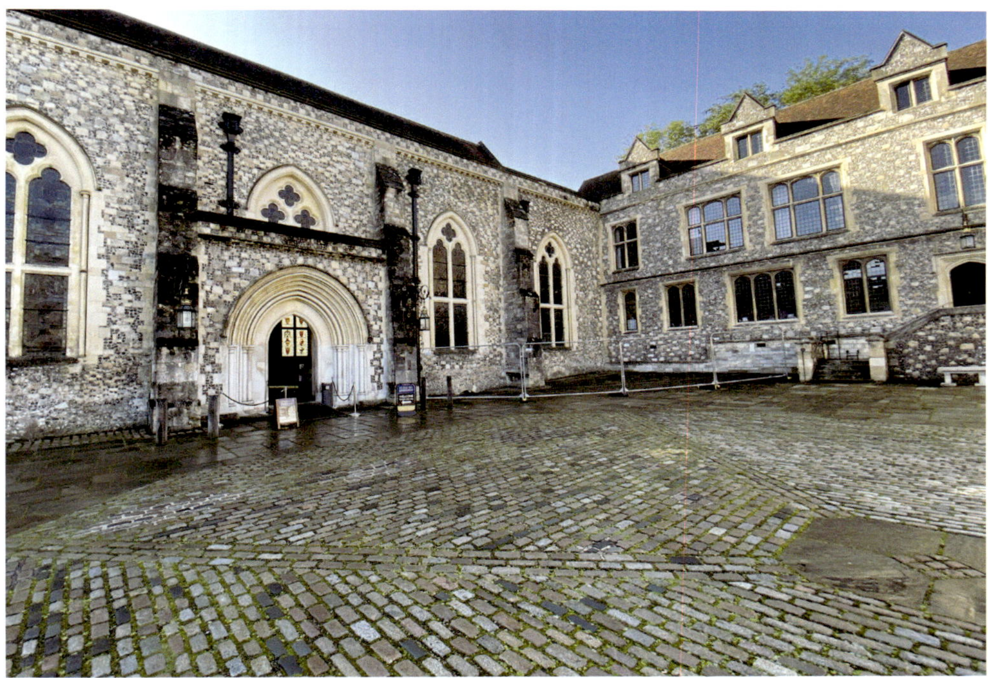

The castle was destroyed by Oliver Cromwell's men in 1645 and only the Great Hall built by Henry III (r. 1216–1272) in 1222 remains. It is one of the earliest Gothic-styled medieval halls.

The death could have been an accident and accidental deaths from hunting were very much an occupational hazard among noblemen of the time. Indeed, King Rufus' own brother, Richard, had also previously died hunting in the New Forest in similar circumstances. He was also buried at Winchester Cathedral and it is believed that his body could also be in the mortuary chests. However, in King Rufus' case many conspiracy theories have been put forward to suggest that the king was killed deliberately.

Tyrrell always proclaimed his innocence, but it has been chronicled that Tyrrell was a renowned shot and was unlikely to have missed his intended target. It has also been noted that Tyrrell had never actually sworn allegiance to the king and was considered to have been the only man in the vicinity of the shooting at the time.

Some say that Tyrrell fired at the king due to their previous evening's quarrel. Others have pointed out that he may have been put up to it by Henry, who had the most to gain from the king's death and indeed, the indecent haste with which he took the crown certainly suggests that it may have been planned and that Tyrrell may have been in the employ of Henry.

The new king, Henry I, like his father, William the Conqueror and his brother, King Rufus, had a reputation for brutality. However, he was considered to be the most educated and most intelligent of the Norman kings.

Did You Know?
Henry I was married to Matilda of Scotland and as a result, King Charles III is directly descended from King Alfred the Great.

Before ascending to the throne, Henry was Count of Cotentin (also known as the Cherbourg Peninsular) and during that time one of the most prominent barons that was answerable to him was his first cousin, Richard de Redvers, who was one of Henry's stalwart supporters in his conflicts against his brother Robert Curthose. He had also served alongside William the Conqueror at the Battle of Hastings in 1066 and was given the manor of Mosterton in Dorset as a result.

Henry ascended to the throne and immediately had Flambard imprisoned in the Tower of London, as the first ever 'guest' of that establishment, an action which would have been met with universal approval in Christchurch. However, Flambard managed to escape by having a barrel of wine delivered to him with a rope inside. He simply got his captors drunk and then used the rope to scale the walls.

Having ousted Flambard, Henry gave Richard de Redvers a great deal of land and estates, making him one of the richest men in the country. Included in this was the principal town or caput of the feudal barony of Plympton, Devon, which included the manor and borough of Christchurch – the so called Honour of Christchurch. It also meant that he had the Lordship of the Isle of Wight including Carisbrooke Castle, as well as many widely scattered manors in several counties. De Redvers then continued to be one of Henry's most trusted barons and advisors and was often Henry's only witness, as he signed more than twenty royal charters.

Meanwhile, Robert disputed Henry's right to be king and as a result, Henry immediately found himself in conflict with his older brother, who he defeated at the Battle of Tinchebray in 1106. After this, Henry was able to include Normandy as a possession of the English Crown and in 1107, Robert was duly imprisoned in the large stone keep at Corfe Castle, which along with other improvements and further consolidation of fortifications was instigated by Henry himself. Robert was then moved to Devizes Castle where he spent the next twenty years, before finally being moved to Cardiff Castle to spend his final years, having been blinded as a punishment for a failed escape attempt.

Henry promised to correct many of William Rufus' unpopular policies. He cultivated better relations with the church and recalled Anslem from exile to re-appoint him as Archbishop of Canterbury. He also introduced courts of law and improved the coinage.

According to the chronicles of history, Henry ruled the country wisely, but of course, he may have had a good write-up, as he had a cooperative relationship with the chroniclers, i.e. the church, unlike his erstwhile brother, Rufus.

The Norman barons ruled England with an iron fist and built some 2,000 castles in England at strategic points, partly for fortification, but mainly to keep order, collect taxes and subjugate the local population.

Therefore, Richard de Redvers expanded and improved Christchurch's defences and enlarged on the original Saxon fortification of Christchurch Castle. He was responsible for the building of the earthen mound or motte and also for the construction of an improved wooden fort on the top. Meanwhile, a thriving community continued to develop around the priory, castle and port.

In 1107, Richard de Redvers died and the Manor of Christchurch passed to his son Baldwin de Redvers. Then in 1118, Henry I's wife, Matilda of Scotland, died at the age of thirty-seven. Two years later, Henry's heirs, William and his younger brother, Richard, drowned in the *White Ship* disaster of 1120, when it went down off the coast of Normandy. Three years after that, Henry married Adeliza of Louvain in the hope of producing another son and heir. However, the marriage produced no children and as a result, in 1127, Henry declared that his daughter, Matilda, would ascend to the throne and had her married off to Geoffrey of Anjou. This news did not go down too well among the barons, as a Norman monarch was required to be a warrior foremost and a monarch second. However, the barons did reluctantly give their oaths to accept Matilda as the next sovereign.

On the death of Henry I in 1135, Stephen of Blois, Matilda's cousin, disregarded his previous oath to accept Matilda as Queen and seized the throne. The majority of barons also followed suit as they were not prepared to have a queen as their monarch and certainly not one who was married to one of their Angerin enemies, Geoffrey of Anjou. However, Matilda was not going to give up the throne lightly and this was the catalyst for a period of civil war known as the Anarchy (1135–1153), during which Matilda invaded England in 1139 while her husband attacked Normandy.

Baldwin de Redvers was a supporter of Matilda and he was made 1st Earl of Devon by her. As a result, Christchurch Castle came under attack from Stephen's supporters and was captured in 1136. However, Baldwin de Redvers then led a force to besiege it and he successfully re-captured it in the same year.

In 1147, during the Anarchy, Baldwin de Redvers joined the Second Crusade and it was rumoured that he had died whilst on the trip prompting one of King Stephen's commanders, Walter de Pinkney, to besiege and capture Christchurch Castle in 1148. De Pinkney then subjected the inhabitants of Christchurch to a torrid time and committed many atrocities, resulting in his eventual ambush and death at the hands of the locals.

The rumours of Baldwin de Redvers' death on the Crusades proved to be greatly exaggerated and it is thought that on his safe return from the Holy Land in 1149, Baldwin was responsible for the addition of the stone keep and the introduction of a bailey, as he further enhanced the defences of the castle. He also had the luxurious Constable's House built adjacent to the castle on the bank of the Mill Stream. The Norman House, as it is also known, is a fine example of Norman domestic architecture and is one of only a few surviving similar buildings in the country.

As the de Redvers family was rarely in residence, the castle tended to be presided over by a bailiff or constable, who lived in the Constable's House, which was generally considered more comfortable to stay in than the castle itself, particularly as it also included the height of medieval luxury: a garderobe.

Did You Know?
A garderobe was the term used to describe a medieval toilet and when King John stayed at Christchurch or Corfe Castle, one of his servant's many unenviable jobs was the task of making sure that the garderobe was in a suitable state for the king's patronage. However, another of the many aspects of a medieval royal servant's life that was distinctly unpleasant was that their quarters were also shared with flea-ridden dogs, which caused the servant's clothes to also become infested. Still happily, this problem was solved by hanging the clothes in the garderobe overnight and allowing the putrid smell to kill the fleas. This practice is where the term wardrobe has arisen from.

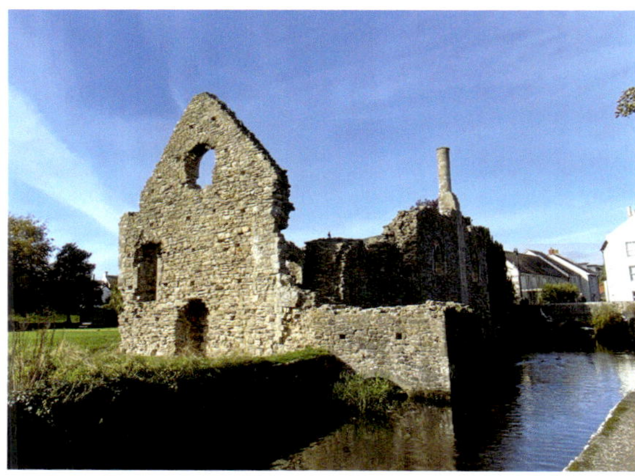

The Constable's House had a garderobe
protruding over the Mill Stream
where the waste could be deposited.

In 1150, Baldwin de Redvers was instrumental in the church at Christchurch becoming an Augustine Priory, then in November 1153, the Anarchy drew to a close when an arrangement was brokered whereby Stephen (r. 1135–1154) would remain king until his death and then be succeeded by Matilda's son, Henry Plantagenet, who became Henry II (r. 1154–1189). Thus the Plantagenet dynasty, which held the throne until the death of Richard III in 1485, was ushered in.

Richard and John were the only two of King Henry II's eight sons who survived him and upon Henry's death, Richard I (r. 1189–1199) was duly crowned. He spent the majority of his time on the Crusades in the Holy Lands and while he was away, his brother managed affairs at home with his associate William Longchamp. Throughout this time, it is thought that John plotted against his brother whilst also having to fend off Robin Hood, who was loyal to King Richard I and robbed from the rich, including tax collectors appointed by John, to give to the poor.

In 1199, Richard I (The Lionheart), was killed by an arrow while laying siege to Chalus in France, allowing John (r. 1199–1216), surely the most evil king ever to be crowned monarch of England, finally to come to power. Immediately on receiving the crown, he set about dealing with a potential threat to the throne in the form of his nephew, Prince Arthur of Brittany, who was the son of his deceased brother Geoffrey. John led an army to Poitou in France and captured the fifteen-year-old Arthur after besieging his fortress, the Castle of Mirabeau.

Arthur was imprisoned at the Chateau de Falaise and guarded by Hubert de Burgh, who was ordered by King John to castrate and blind the prisoner. Hubert refused to comply with this brutal and malicious order, so King John personally tied a heavy weight to Arthur's body and dropped him into the River Seine and drowned him.

Another potential threat to the throne, Arthur's sister, Eleanor, the Maid of Brittany, was also taken prisoner and brought back to Corfe Castle along with twenty-five French knights. Eleanor was well treated and had William's, the King of Scotland's, daughters, who were also John's prisoners, to share her captivity with. She was imprisoned in Corfe until 1222, before spending further periods of captivity at Gloucester, Marlborough and Bristol, where she died. The twenty-five French knights didn't fare so well though; they were simply thrown in a dungeon at Corfe Castle and left to starve to death.

During his seventeen-year reign, King John was a frequent visitor to Christchurch, which was in an ideal location between Corfe Castle, one of the premiere strongholds in the land, and the important city of Winchester. He enjoyed the luxury of the Constable's House and its garderobe whilst also taking the opportunity to hunt in the New Forest.

Meanwhile the priory was completed in 1234.

Baldwin de Redvers died childless in 1269, meaning his widow, Margaret of Savoy, inherited Christchurch Castle along with the lordship of the Isle of Wight, which she held until her death in 1292, when the estate was inherited by Baldwin's sister, Isabella de Fortibus. King Edward I (r. 1272–1307) was keen to buy Christchurch Castle and the lordship of the Isle of Wight from her and supposedly arrived just in time at her death bed in 1293 to hear her grant this to him. Fortuitously, of course, the only witness to this was Edward himself. Then in 1299, Edward I handed the estate to his wife, Margaret, who was the daughter of King Phillip III of France.

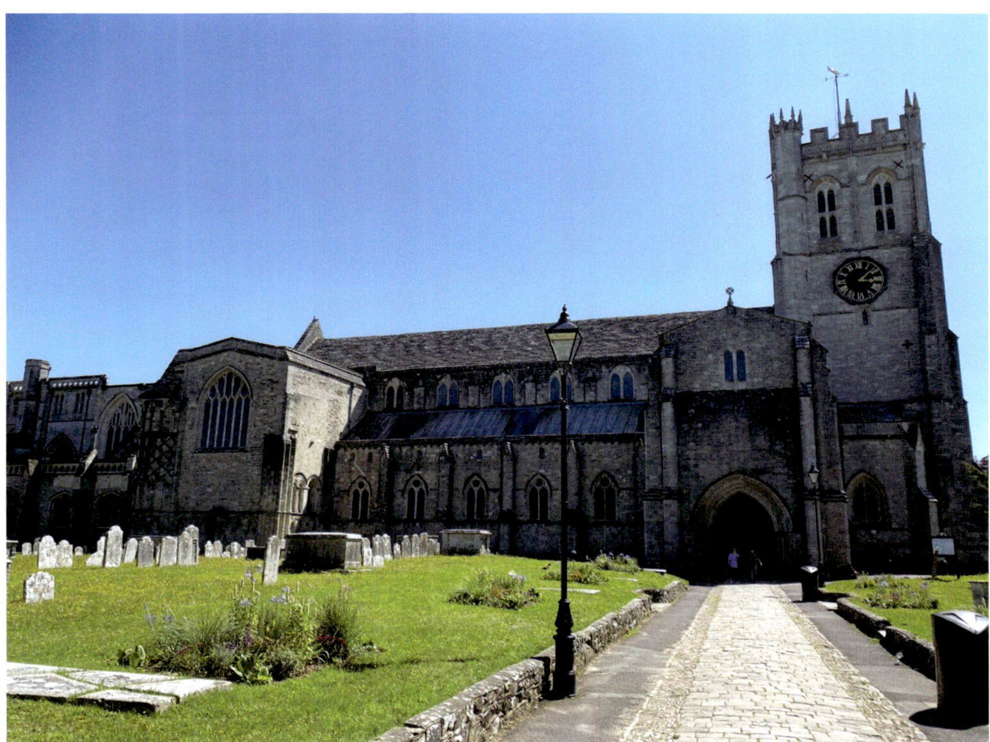

Christchurch Priory.

Thirty-one years later, Edward III (r. 1327–1377) gave the castle to William Montague, who later became the Earl of Salisbury. The castle then passed through the hands of successive generations of that family, until its demise in the English Civil War (1642–1651) (*see* The English Civil War (1642–1651) and the Battle for Christchurch).

Did You Know that?
A widely held misconception is that ducking stools were used to identify and punish witches. In fact, they were never used for this purpose in Britain. Instead, they were used to punish and publicly humiliate scolds (women who were found guilty of verbal abuse, brawling and general anti-social behaviour). The offender received as many duckings as was decreed by her sentence.

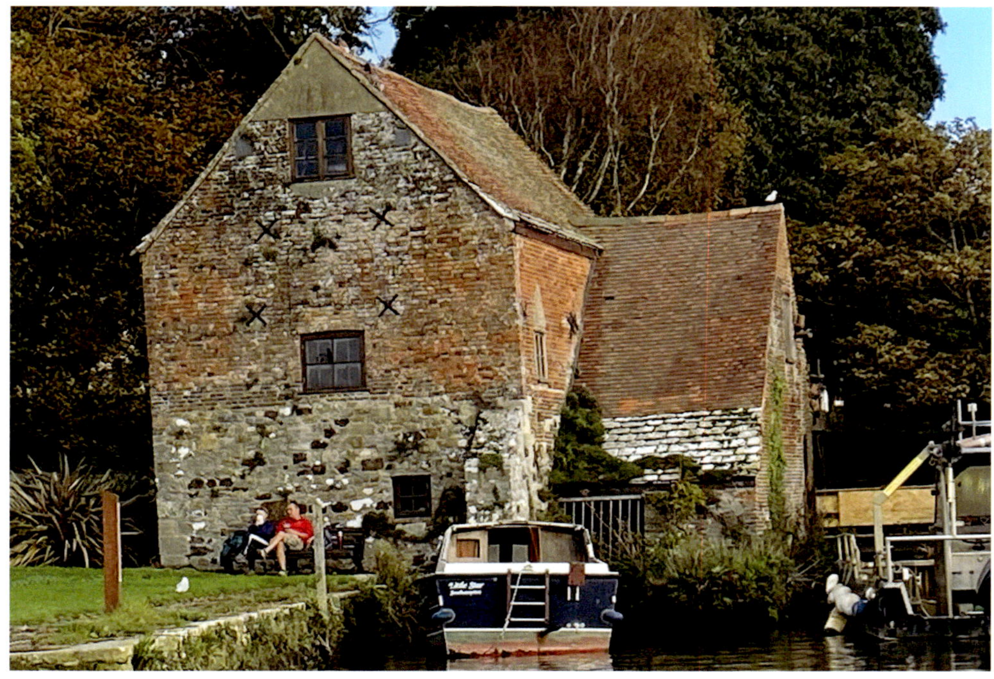

Place Mill dates from the eleventh century.

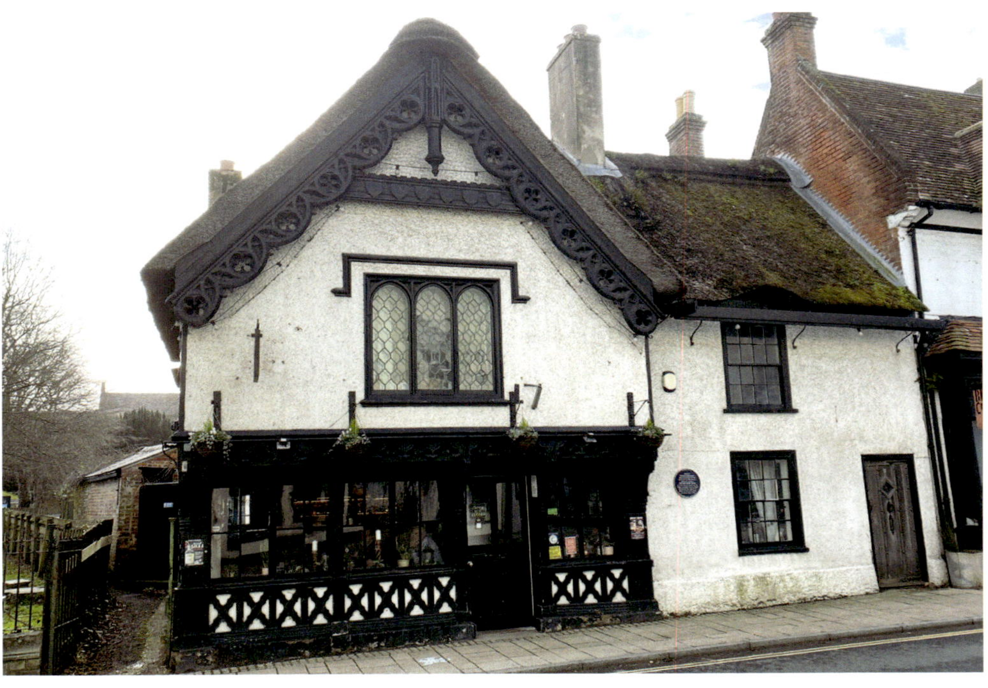

The Old Court House was built in the twelfth century and is now Dirty Gerties Gin Parlour.

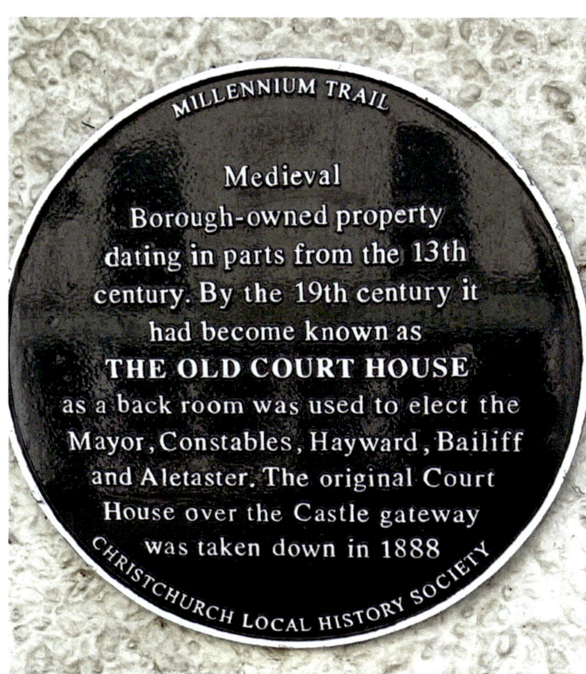

Plaque – The Old Court House.

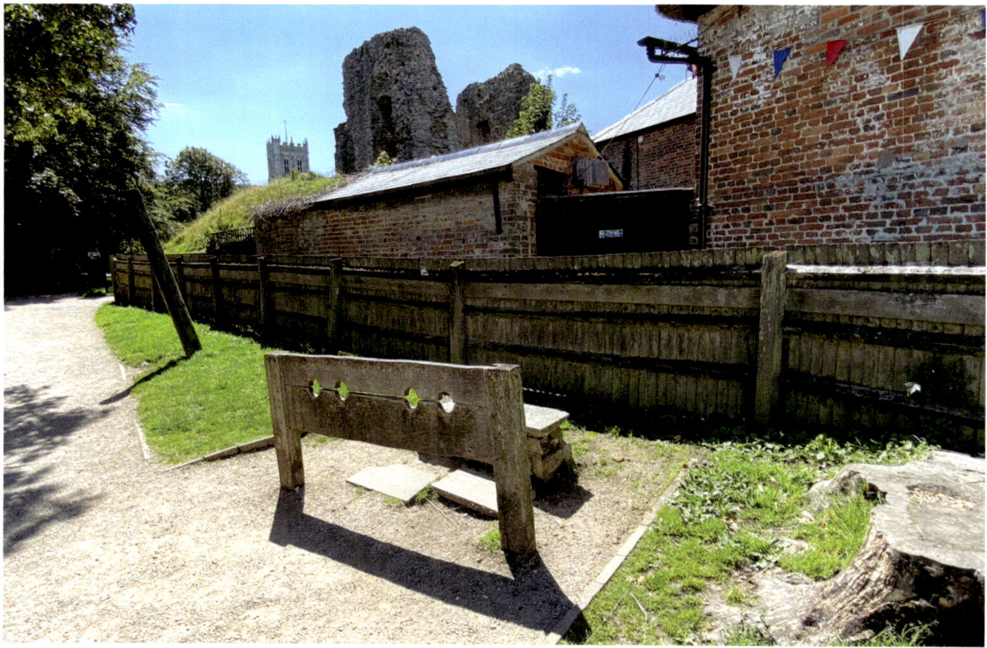

A pillory was a form of stocks where miscreants were held within a wooden framework with holes for their head and hands, so they could be pinioned whilst being exposed to public ridicule and abuse.

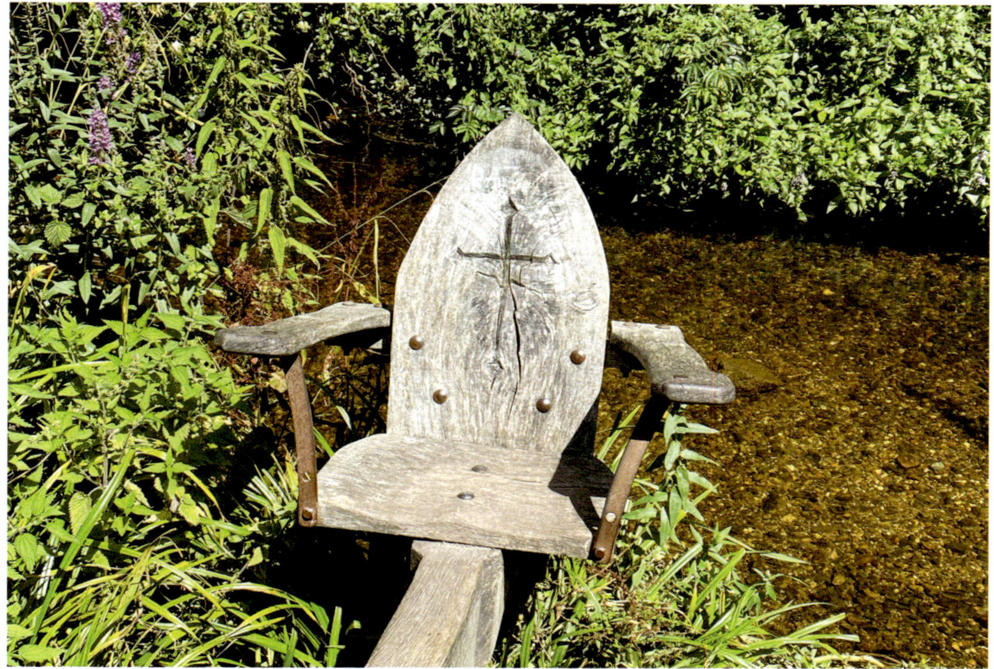

Ducking stool.

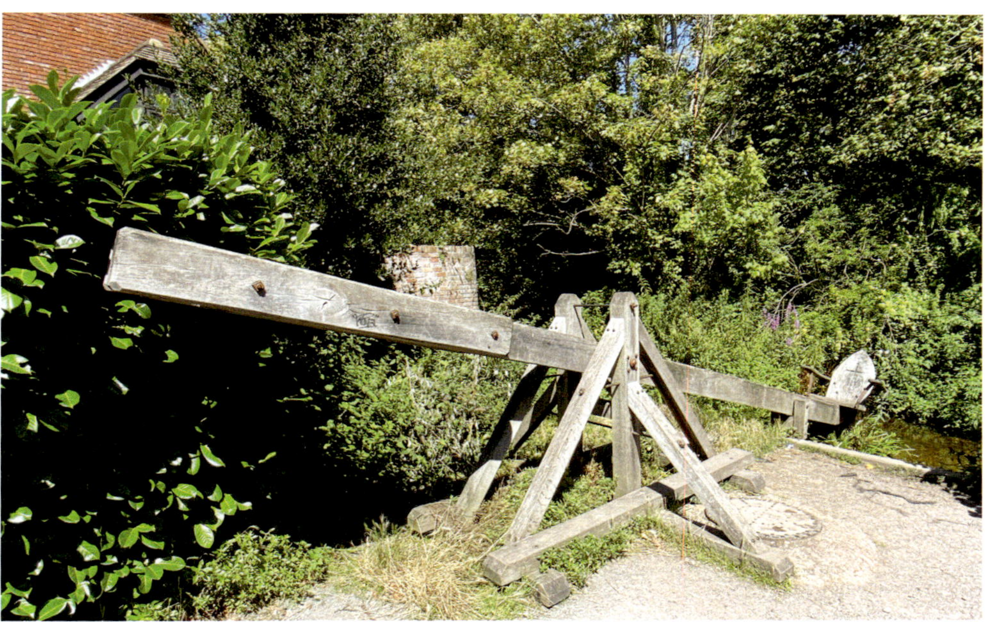

The ducking stool was placed in situ in 1986. It is a replica, but is close to the original site of one that was in use from 1350 until 1807. The Mill Stream has silted up considerably and was much wider and deeper when the original chair was in place.

2. The English Civil War (1642–1651) and the Battle for Christchurch

Charles I (r. 1625–1649) believed in the 'Divine Right of the Monarchy' and didn't take kindly to advice from a Parliament, now dominated by Protestant Puritans who were opposed to the supremacy of the Monarch in religion. He had also further antagonised his Protestant Puritan detractors by marrying a French Catholic princess, Henrietta Maria (1609–1669), who was the youngest daughter of King Henry IV of France and Marie de Medici. She was born at the Hotel du Louvre in Paris and became the mother of Charles II and James II. However, when Charles was coroneted at Westminster Abbey on 2 February 1626, she was not crowned queen at this ceremony due to her Catholicism.

Charles is said to have approved of the marriage, but that didn't stop a number of infidelities with various mistresses, making the early years of their marriage difficult. However, the couple did go on to develop a close relationship, in which she involved herself in her husband's attempts to overthrow Parliament and further antagonised many by seeking to enlist support for the king from the Pope, as well as overtly practising the Catholic religion herself.

The resultant religious tensions eventually erupted into a series of conflicts known as the Wars of the Three Kingdoms, which took place in Scotland, England and Ireland from 1639 to 1651. These wars consisted of the Bishops' Wars (1639 and 1640), the Irish Confederate Wars (1641–1653), the First English Civil War (1642–1646), the Second English Civil War (1648), the Third English Civil War (1649–1651) and the Cromwellian Conquest of Ireland (1649–1653).

As far as the First English Civil War was concerned (1642–1646), King and Parliament were at loggerheads and when Charles I decided to have five of the leading parliamentary Puritans arrested, he precipitated the conflict, which pitched the Protestant, Puritan and Parliamentarian Roundheads, led by Oliver Cromwell, against the predominantly Catholic Royalist Cavaliers.

At this time, the majority of English people supported the institution of the monarchy, but the issue was whether the monarchy or Parliament had ultimate power. Those who supported Charles I in his claim of the 'Divine Right of Kings' and the monarch's superiority over Parliament and the Church were known as Royalists, while their Parliamentarian opponents were more in favour of a constitutional monarchy.

Initially, the Royalists enjoyed great success, securing victory at the Battle of Edgehill (1642), which put the Parliamentarians on the back foot. However, in 1643 the Covenanter Scots, led by Archibald Campbell, 9th Earl of Argyll, Chief of the powerful Clan Campbell, advocated civil and religious union with England as the best way to preserve a Presbyterian Kirk. They made an agreement called the Solemn League and Covenant, in which the Scottish Covenanters agreed to offer military support to the English Parliamentarians.

The combined force of English Parliamentarians and Scottish Covenanters then won a series of battles in 1644, and, most significantly, the Battle of Marston Moor on 2 July 1644. As a result, the tide of the Civil War started to turn in favour of the Parliamentarians. Indeed, by the end of 1644, both local Royalist strongholds of Christchurch Castle and Corfe Castle had been besieged by the Parliamentarians.

Did You Know?
Christchurch, Wimborne and Corfe Castle were the only Royalist strongholds in the area, and were surrounded by Parliamentary towns, such as Poole, Wareham and Southampton.

Mary Bankes and her supporters managed to repel the Parliamentarian invaders at Corfe Castle, but then a detatchment of some 2,000 Roundhead cavalry under Sir William Waller turned their attention to Christchurch, taking the Royalist troops defending the town by surprise. The Parliamentarians went on to capture 100 horse and 400 foot soldiers and took control of the castle and town. Waller's men even had the audacity to stable their horses in the priory.

In early January 1645, Lord George Goring, Governor of Portsmouth and a strong Royalist supporter, led a force of 1,000 Royalist Cavaliers to Christchurch. The Parliamentarians in Christchurch were now under the command of Major Phillip Lower and those who hadn't managed to take refuge in the castle or priory fled the town for the safe Parliamentary haven of Hurst Castle, near Milford on Sea opposite the Isle of Wight. Goring then laid siege to Christchurch Castle, but eventually withdrew, having come to the conclusion that his force was insufficient and that he lacked the siege guns required to take it. However, he returned on 15 January 1645 with a larger army and the appropriate siege-busting heavy-calibre artillery.

In the meantime, Lower's Parliamentarian troops within the castle had strengthened their defensive position and those that had previously escaped to Hurst Castle had also returned. Accordingly, a fierce three-day battle ensued, during which houses were demolished on the corner of Church Street and Castle Street in order to provide room for the besieging army of Royalists to place their cannons and also to remove obstacles from their field of fire.

However, the Royalists were still struggling to regain the castle and were suffering heavy losses in the attempt. Consequently, when news reached them that larger parliamentary forces were nearby in Lymington and were heading towards Christchurch, they were forced to abort the siege. The Royalist withdrawal then allowed the Parliamentarians to retain the castle and re-take the town, which they then held onto for the duration of the war.

Nevertheless, the civil war continued in other theatres and in February 1645, the Parliamentarians founded England's first professional army, 'The New Model Army', and this was a major factor in the Parliamentarian's increasing their ascendancy, as they went on to achieve further success, at the Battle of Naseby in June 1645, and then turned their attention again to the important stronghold of Corfe Castle, which continued to be the only Royalist castle still holding out between Exeter and London.

This time they arrived at Corfe with more men and more military hardware than the first siege. However as before, the castle continued to withstand the onslaught, despite the Parliamentarians setting up cannon emplacements in the nearby church of St Edward the Martyr and the Rings, which were the remains of a fortification originally built by Stephen to attack the castle during the Anarchy (*see* Christchurch's Medieval Connection). However, the heavy bombardment and the starvation conditions were beginning to take their toll on the besieged and after seven weeks, loyalty was beginning to waver in some quarters. Colonel Pitman left the castle on the pretence that he was going to return with Royalist reinforcements. Instead, he secretly made a deal with Colonel Bingham, the Parliamentarian commander, and returned under the cover of darkness on 27 February 1646 with 120 Parliamentarian troops from nearby Lulworth Castle. They were disguised as Royalists and thus gained entrance to the castle and occupied the stronghold from within, which in turn forced Lady Bankes to surrender, finally putting an end to the Corfe Castle siege.

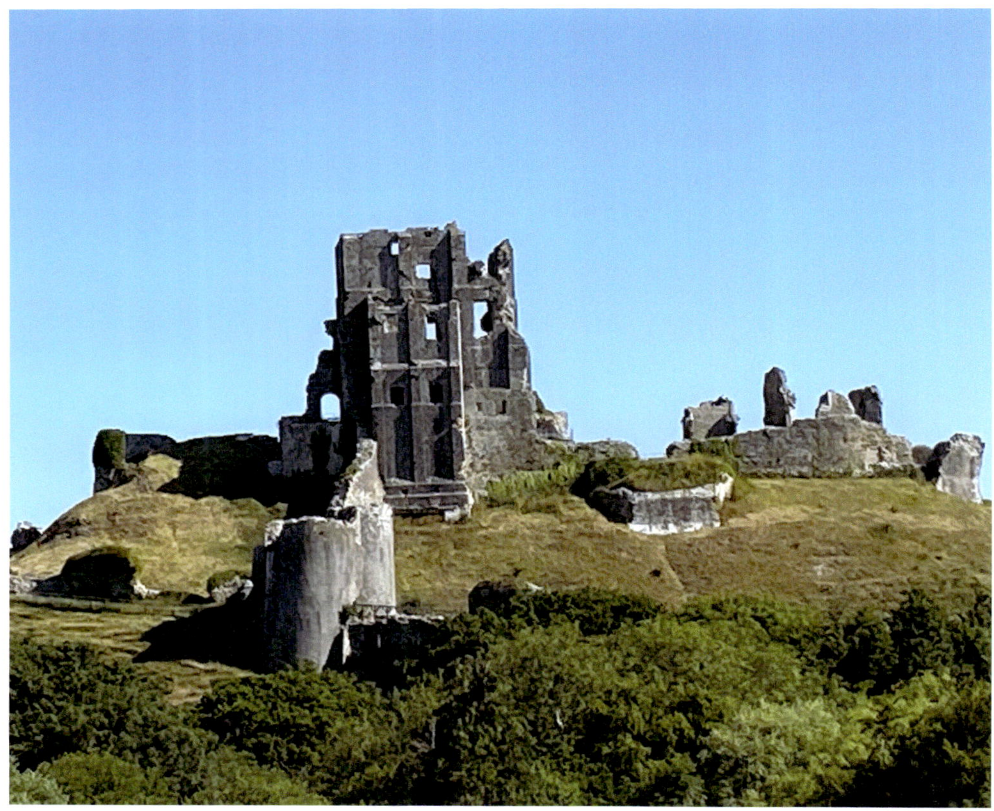

Corfe Castle.

The Parliamentarians allowed the garrison and Lady Bankes to leave unharmed and then ceremoniously presented her with the castle keys in recognition of her bravery. The keys were only of sentimental value though, as shortly after the castle's capture, senior figures from the town of Poole petitioned Parliament to demolish the castle and fine Lady Bankes. They felt that the poor inhabitants of Poole and other towns in Dorset who had supported Parliament should receive some compensation for the hardship they had suffered during the Civil War.

Poole had supported the Parliamentarians, mainly because the wealthy merchants who had become rich due to the trade with Newfoundland were against the ship money tax imposed by Charles I and were also not very happy with the lack of protection from pirates afforded by the Crown.

Parliament subsequently ordered the demolition of the castle and a team of Sappers (engineers) set about destroying it with the aid of gunpowder – hence the state we see it in today. However, the destruction of Corfe Castle did have one bonus for the villagers in that it provided a ready-made supply of building material and even today some houses in the village still possess this original stone.

Meanwhile, Cromwell evicted those members of Parliament that were against trying the king for treason and formed the Rump Parliament, which duly tried Charles, resulting in his execution on 30 January 1649.

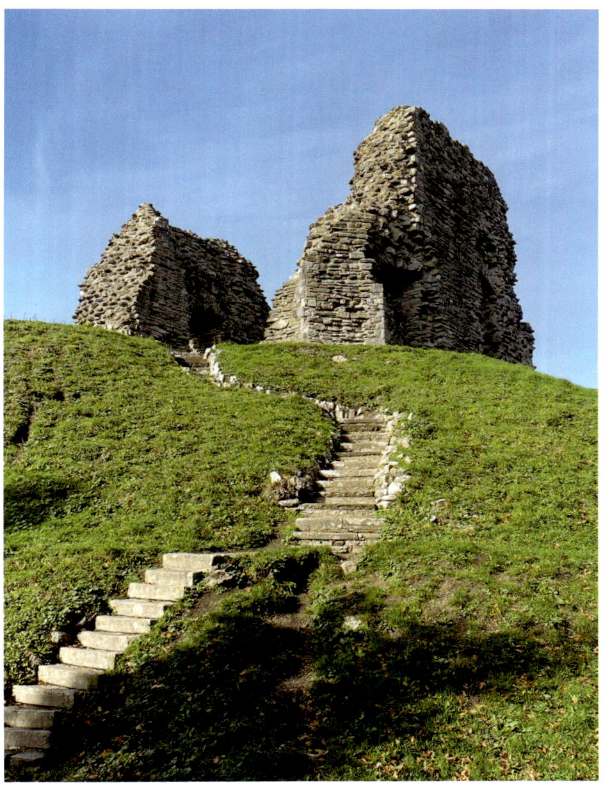

Christchurch Castle.

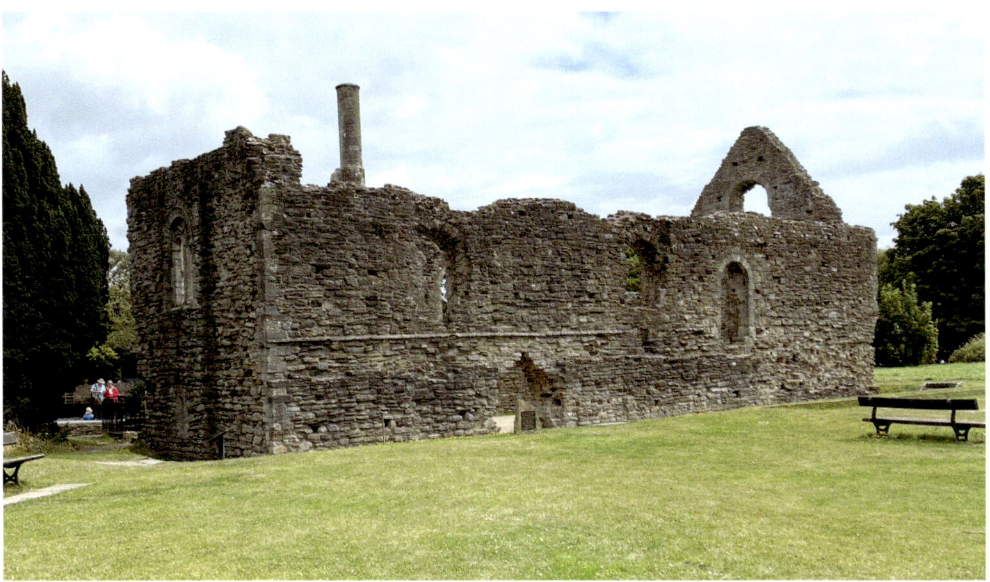

The Constable's House or Norman House depicted here is one of only two aspects of Christchurch Castle that remain since Cromwell's destruction; the other is the motte and bailey.

In 1650, the Parliamentarians ordered Christchurch Castle, which still had its battery of cannons intact, to be slighted (destroyed) as Cromwell still feared the stronghold's potential potency should the Royalists recapture it in an attempt to put Charles I's son, Charles II, on the throne.

As at Corfe Castle, local Christchurch people also utilised the stone for their own building purposes and by the late seventeenth century, the once proud castle was basically a ruin, with only the motte and bailey surviving. However, the Constable's Hall remained intact as it was excluded from the demolition orders.

Did You Know?
Major Phillip Lower was promoted to Lieutenant Colonel and appointed Governor of Winchester for his valiant defence of Christchurch against a Royalist force five times larger than his.

Cromwell died on 3 September 1658 and was succeeded by his son, Richard, who soon found himself unsuited for government. A chaotic period ensued during which he was unable to control the warring factions of the army and Parliament. In May 1659, he was ordered to resign by the army, and Prince Charles I's exiled son was invited by Parliament to ascend the throne as Charles II (r. 1660–1685).

3. Smuggling

In the sixteenth, seventeenth, eighteenth and nineteenth centuries, peaking between 1770 and 1815, many coastlines abounded with smugglers. There were mitigating factors to these activities, as it was a time when high taxes were sought to finance wars and the imposition of duty on imported goods significantly raised prices beyond the pocket of many. Therefore, smuggling was seen by some as a necessity for survival, and even those not actively concerned in the 'trade' – as smuggling was euphemistically termed – tended to turn a blind eye.

Christchurch was heavily involved as the unique location at the confluence of the rivers Stour and Avon allied to the adjacent Stanpit Marsh, with its deep-water channels and tall reeds, made the area a veritable smuggler's paradise.

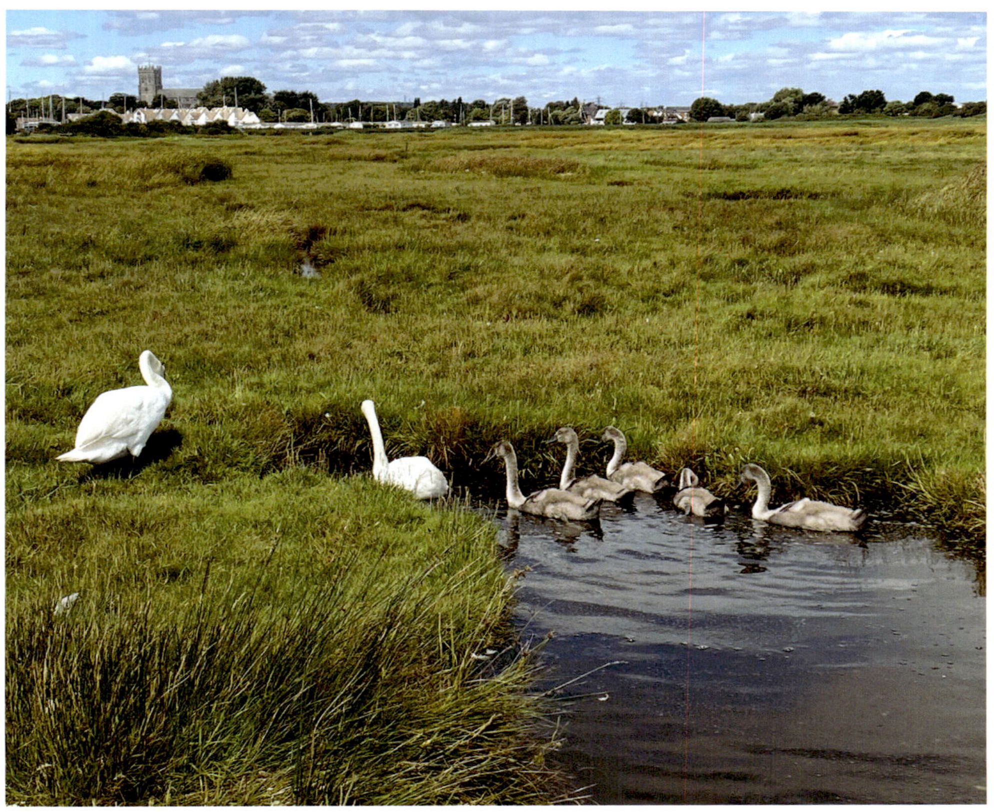

A family of swans at Stanpit Marsh.

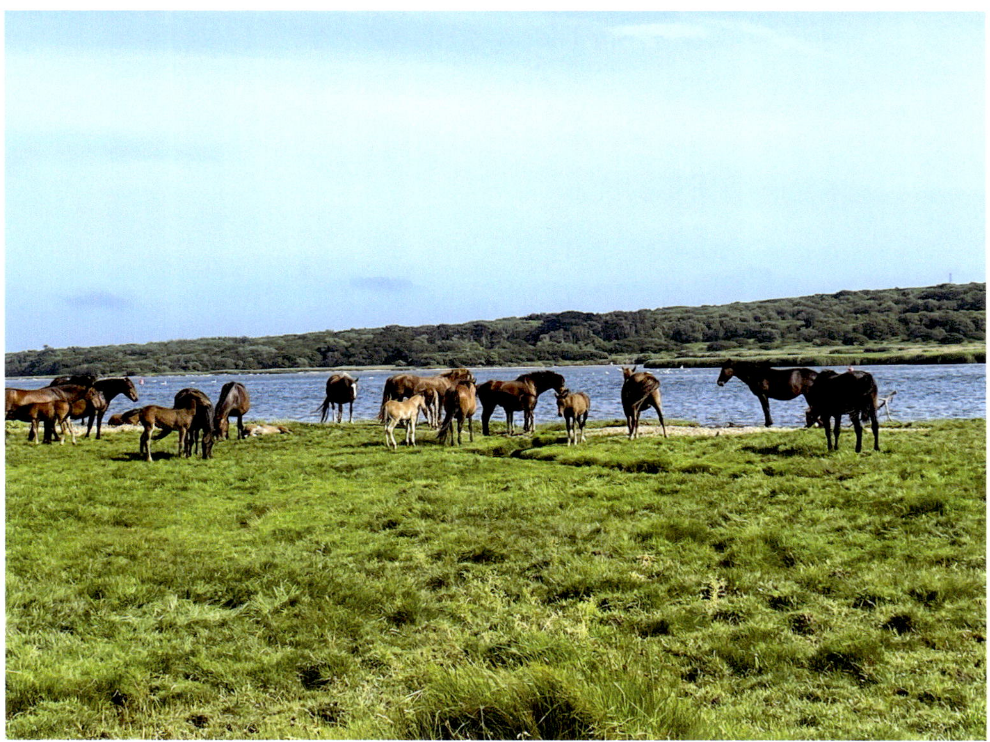

New Forest ponies at Stanpit Marsh.

The prolific concealment of contraband such as tobacco, wine and tea, for which there was always a great demand, resulted in many of the gang leaders becoming very wealthy on the proceeds. However, by the 1850s, the effect of the return of peace after the Napoleonic Wars, along with tax reductions and a more efficient coastguard and customs, made the operations less viable, all but destroying the practice.

Once the smugglers had negotiated the fast-flowing water and dangerous currents, known as the 'Run', created by the narrow gap between Mudeford Sandspit and Mudeford Quay, they had access to Stanpit Marsh and the confluence of the Stour and Avon rivers. Navigating the Run was a test of seamanship and was made even more treacherous because the sandbanks in the vicinity could shift overnight. This was an advantage to the smugglers though, as they tended to be very skilled seamen and the revenue men less so.

The smuggled goods could then be hidden or stored locally, or transported further afield via Bourne Heath, which in those days stretched from Poole to Christchurch and beyond to Fordingbridge.

The smuggling activity in the Christchurch area reached an explosive climax when a smuggler's vessel full of contraband, named *Civil Usage*, was sailing in the English Channel towards Christchurch. En route, she sighted a pursuing revenue cutter, *Rose*, so changed course and ran for Cherbourg. She managed to outrun the *Rose* and once in Cherbourg her cargo of contraband was swiftly switched to aggregate.

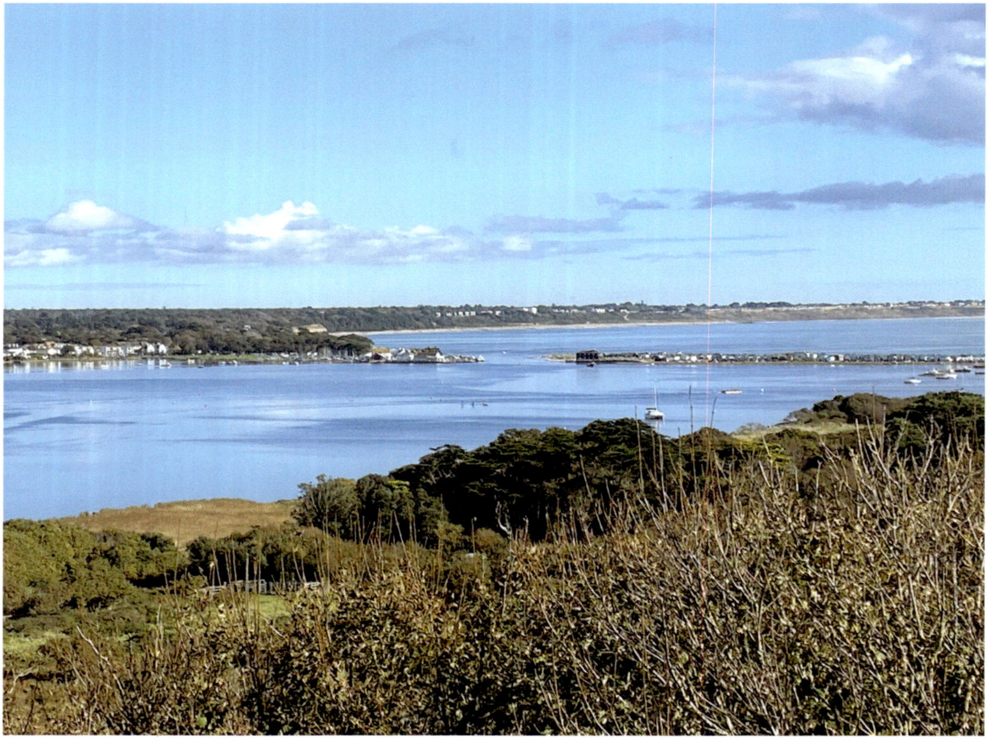

The Run, as the narrow gap between Mudeford Sandspit and Mudeford Quay is known.

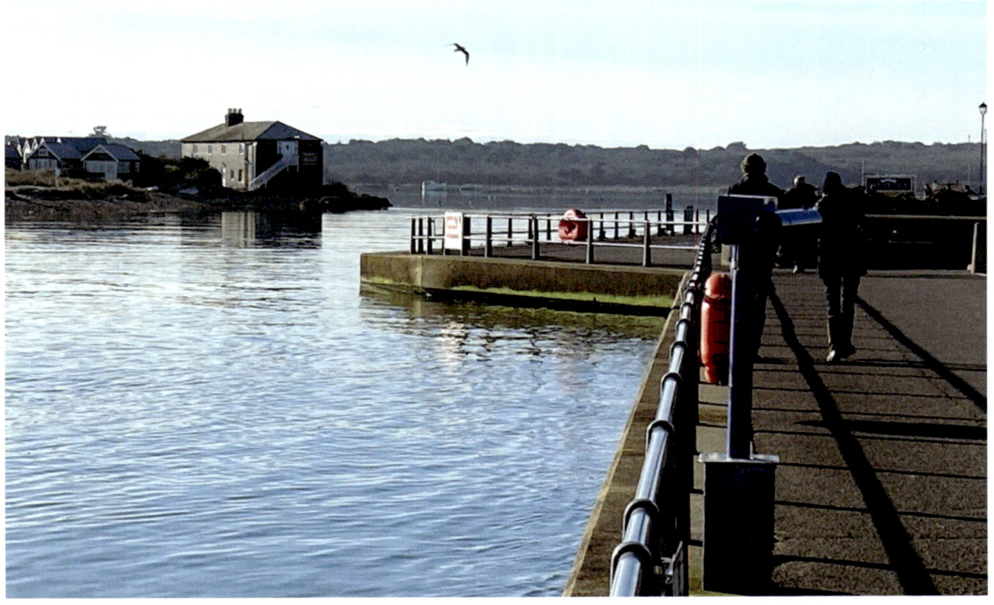

A closer view of the Run.

The *Civil Usage* then returned to Christchurch and as she approached, she was boarded by Revenue Tide Waiters, whose job it was to wait on the tide to check the cargo of incoming suspect vessels. They were obviously unable to find any illicit goods, so the craft was allowed to continue into Christchurch Harbour.

Having successfully completed this feint manoeuvre and sowed the seed in the customs officer's minds that the vessel was perfectly legitimate, the crew of the *Civil Usage* then laid low in Christchurch for a few days, before setting off back to Cherbourg to collect the original illicit cargo, this time accompanied by another smuggling cutter, the *Phoenix*.

Meanwhile the owner of both vessels, smuggling gang leader John Streeter, who was friends with Hannah Seller, the landlady of the notorious smuggler's den of inequity, the Haven House Inn on Mudeford Quay, made preparations for his men to receive a massive haul of contraband. He mustered 300 men, 100 wagons and 400 horses around the smuggler's favoured landing spot of Avon Beach, as the smugglers again approached Christchurch.

However, the build-up of shifty-looking characters in the vicinity didn't go unnoticed by customs and a young excise officer named Noyce alerted his superior, Joshua Jeans, who promptly told him to shut up and go away.

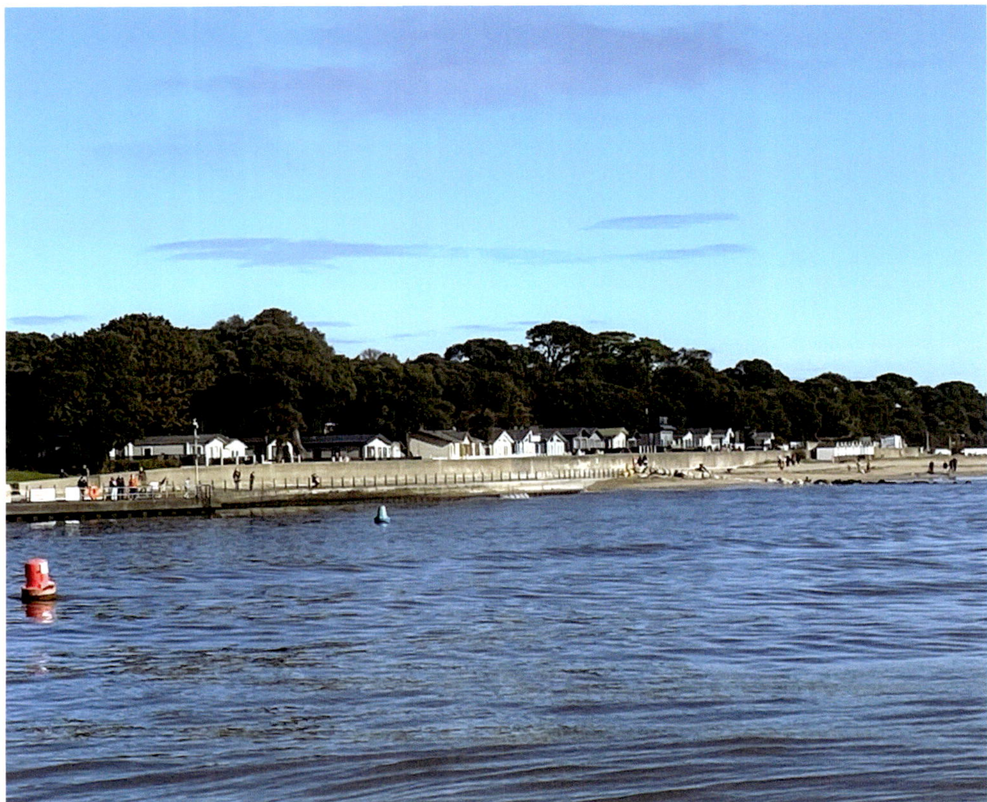

Avon Beach from the sea.

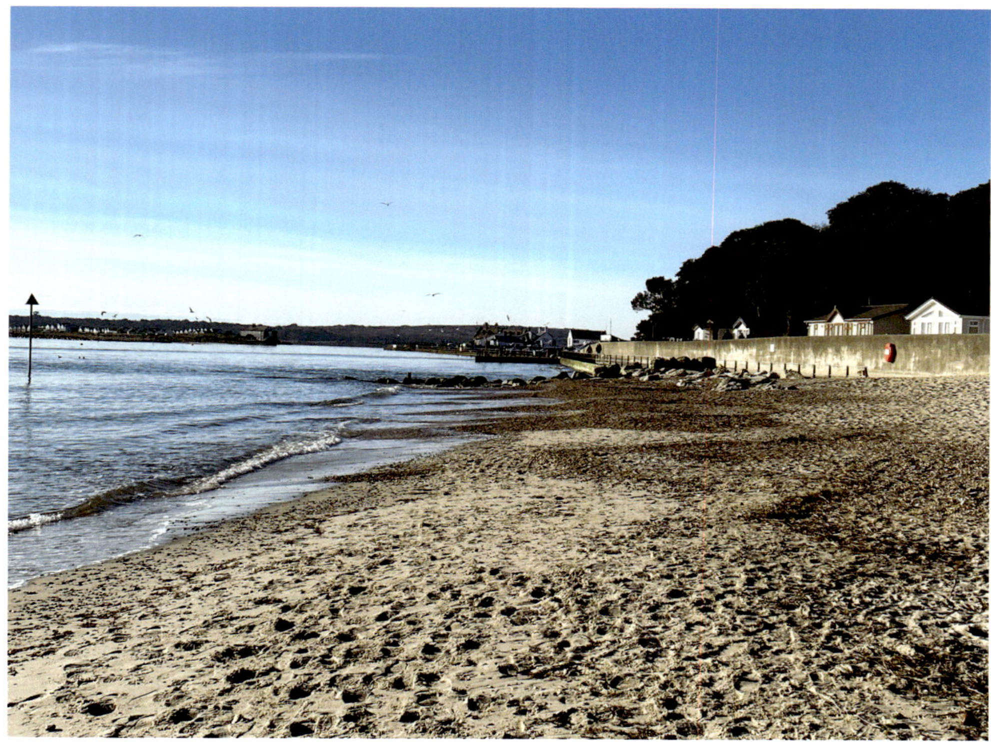

Avon Beach.

A little while later, the crew of revenue cutter the *Resolution*, who were severely outnumbered and powerless to intervene, watched in disbelief as the largest haul of contraband ever landed from a single run, including 6,000 casks of spirits and 400 chests of tea, was unloaded under the supervision of John Streeter. The smuggler's carts then moved off with the booty towards the heath and forest, but as they did so, the *Resolution* dispatched the ship's longboat, which managed to locate and gain assistance from the *Swan* in Poole Bay and the eighteen-gun Royal Naval Sloop HMS *Orestes* just off the Isle of Wight.

On 15 July 1784, the confrontation, which became known as the Battle of Mudeford, reached its zenith when the preventative ships made haste and reached the harbour entrance at around 1800 hours, in effect trapping the smuggler's vessels within the harbour. Captain Ellis of the *Orestes* then dispatched six rowing boats from his craft, all containing armed sailors and marines.

William Allen, the twenty-five-year-old Master of HMS *Orestes* led the naval raiding party with the intention of capturing the smuggler's vessels and towing them out to sea. However, as they drew nearer, they were met with a fusillade of bullets from the smugglers hiding behind the sandbanks of Avon Beach. The preventative men returned fire, but they were at a disadvantage as they were firing from the unstable platform of a rocking boat. Meanwhile, John Streeter rode along the quayside and forced all the customers out of the Haven House Inn to assist in stripping the smugglers' cutters of their lines and rigging.

Many of the smugglers then retreated to the familiar sanctuary of Hannah Seller's Haven House Inn where they holed themselves up in readiness for a gun fight while others continued to fire from the sandbanks of Avon Beach.

As Allen's rowing boat approached the harbour entrance, it became stuck on a sandbank, and as Allen and his crew tried to free it, he was hit and wounded by a gun shot. Despite this setback, the preventative men's assault persisted and they continued returning fire as they rowed up the Run and into the harbour before eventually managing to board the two smuggler's ships and put them out of action. A full-scale shoot-out then raged for five hours and the bombardment also included cannon fire from HMS *Orestes*.

While the smugglers in the Haven House Inn held the customs men at bay, the majority of the contraband was still being moved inland as smugglers melted away into the darkness with their estimated haul of 120,000 gallons of liquor and 25 tons of tea. Meanwhile, Allen's condition was deteriorating and as the preventative forces had by now suffered many other casualties, the assault party had to abandon their attack and retreat back through the Run. Nevertheless, the sailors and revenue men returned the next morning, to successfully seize the smuggler's vessels and tow them away to Cowes on the Isle of Wight.

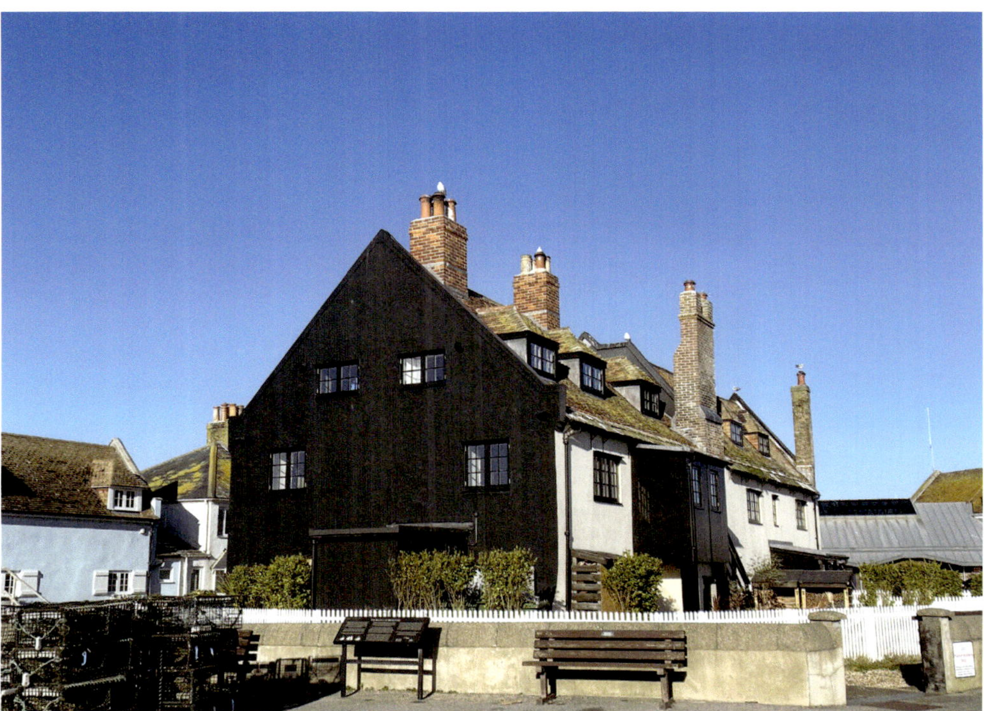

The Old Custom's House was the site of the original Haven House Inn, which had been in existence since 1699 and at the time of the Battle of Mudeford was the only building on the quay.

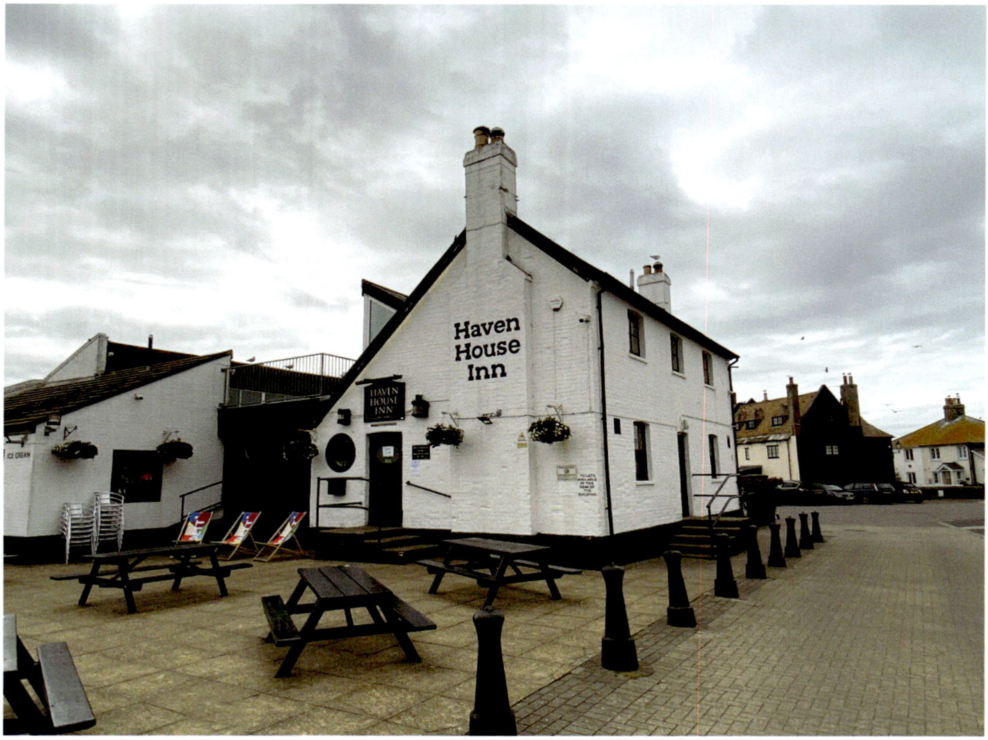

The current Haven House Inn.

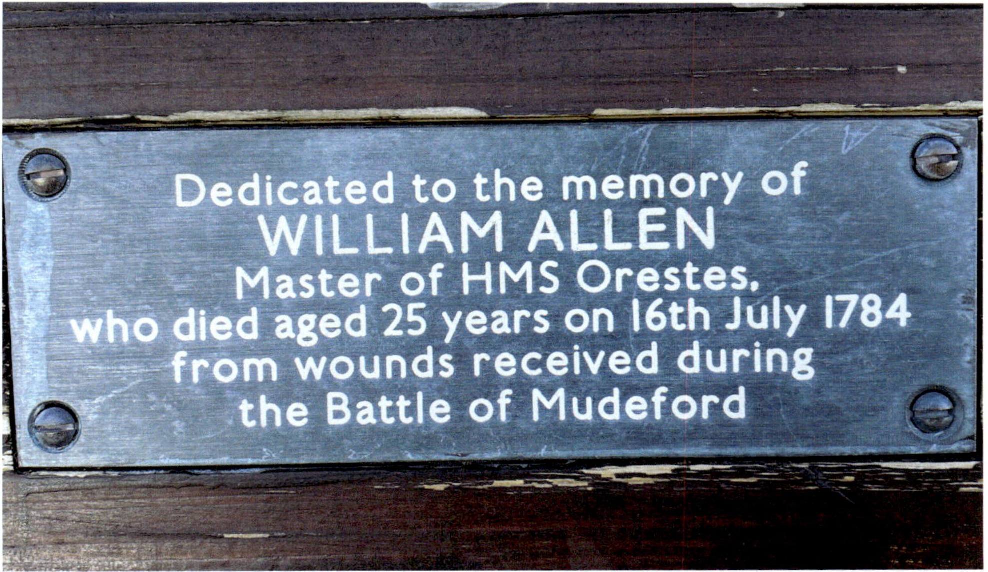

A plaque on a memorial bench to William Allen outside the Old Custom House (formerly the Haven House Inn).

Allen's wound turned out to be fatal and three smugglers were later arrested for his murder. However, two were released through lack of evidence and the only man successfully convicted of the crime was George Coombes, who was hanged at Execution Dock, Wapping, London. His corpse was then returned to Mudeford to be hung in a gibbet, which were iron cages where bodies of those that had been hanged – or body parts from those that had been hanged, drawn and quartered – were put on public display as a deterrent to others.

Another consequence of the battle was that the notorious Haven House Inn was closed down by the authorities, and to add insult to injury for the majority of the former regulars, it was turned into a Customs House, in order to keep a watch over smuggling vessels coming through the Run (the present public house of the same name was a later addition to the quay). The conduct of the revenue men also came under scrutiny after the battle, as although the majority were honest, the lead-up to the battle had shown that there were also plenty that were not.

HM Coastguard was formed by combining the Preventative Water Guard, Riding Officers and Customs Officers and its main role was to combat smuggling. The chief weapon at their disposal locally was an armed cutter which patrolled the sea between Portland and the Isle of Wight.

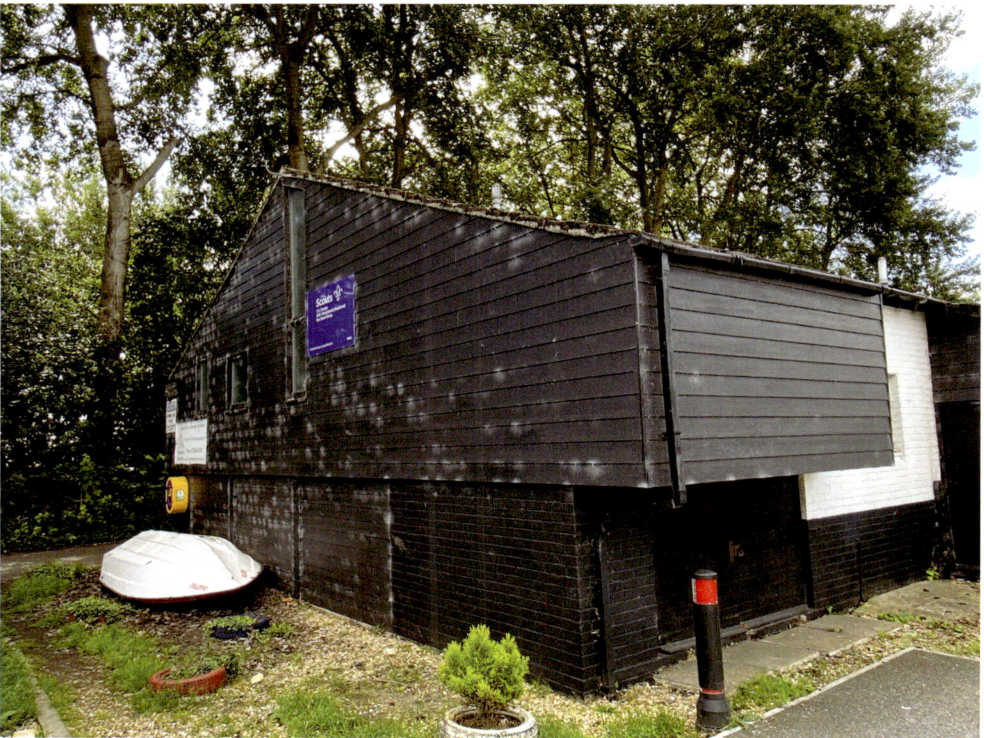

Today the scout hut on Stanpit Recreation Ground is named Orestes in memory of the Royal Naval sloop that was involved in the Battle of Mudeford.

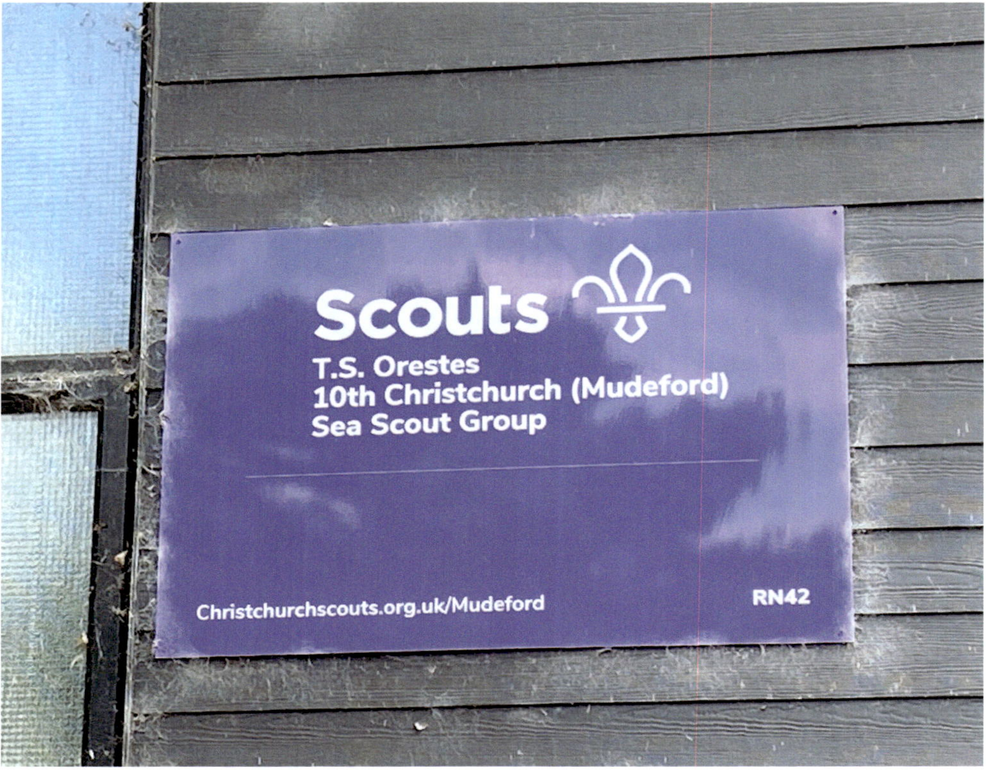

The scout hut sign.

The Riding Officers were usually local men and were generally underpaid and ripe for being corrupted by smugglers, who in many cases were well known to them. They often had an arrangement whereby they confiscated a token amount of contraband in order to claim a successful operation and in return allowed the smugglers to land the bulk of their haul, whilst they also received a percentage of the illicit goods from the smugglers.

Richard Warner attended Grammar School at St Michael's Loft at the top of Christchurch Priory during 1776, from where he had a grandstand view of the town. The revelations of what he saw from his elevated perch of the schoolroom window featured in his autobiography, *Literary Recollections*, and have provided an illuminating insight into eighteenth-century Christchurch life and in particular of the vast scale of the smuggling that was occurring at the time. He wrote:

The revenue troop who had always intelligence of the run, were, it is true, present on these occasions, but with no other views and intentions, than those of perfect peace.

A flood of homely jokes were poured upon them by the passing ruffians; but these were always accompanied by a present of kegs greater or less according to the quantity of smuggled goods; a voluntary toll received, as it was conferred in perfect good humour and with mutual satisfaction.

There is a window in the St Michael's Loft of the priory where it is reputed that a candle was lit to inform smugglers that it was safe to bring their contraband ashore. The window and candle can still be seen today, although who lit the candle is not apparent. It has also been suggested that the loft was a place of storage of contraband.

Warner also describes how this high schoolroom allowed himself and his fellow pupils to view the smugglers in action on Hengistbury Head. He wrote:

> The shore of the noble promontory, Hengistbury Head, at the southern end of the extremity of the united Avon and Stour rivers was a spot frequently chosen as a loading place for the contraband goods.

He goes on to say:

> I have myself seen more than once, a procession of twenty or thirty wagons loaded with kegs of spirits, an armed man sitting at the front and tail of each and surrounded by a troop of two or three hundred horsemen, everyone carrying on his enormous saddle, from two to four tubs of spirits, winding deliberately and with the most picturesque and imposing effect along the skirts of Hengistbury Head on their way towards the wild country north west of Christchurch, the point of their separation.

Warner also mentions a smuggler called Slippery Rogers who, as his name suggests, was an elusive character who repeatedly avoided capture, despite the prolific nature of his nefarious activities and the huge open-decked smuggling vessel which he used. He was believed to have been a descendant of a former Christchurch mayor, Henry Rogers, whose tomb lies within Christchurch Priory churchyard and contains a curious inscription: 'Here we ten are one'.

Warner also recounts that the smugglers were good humoured if things were going their way, but could be absolutely brutal if things were not. For instance, he recounts a tale in his book whereby John Bursey, an honest customs man and the father of one of Warner's fellow pupils in St Michael's Loft, had a visit in the early hours. He answered some loud banging at his door, leaving his wife and children upstairs in bed. Upon answering the door he was viciously assaulted and later died of his injuries. Despite a handsome reward, no one was ever charged with his murder.

Bursey's son, Warner's old school pal, joined the Customs Service himself just in time for the Battle of Mudeford. Unfortunately investigations into the skirmish subsequently found that Riding Officer John Bursey (Junior) had received 100 casks of spirits from the smugglers only a few hours earlier under the orders of his totally corrupt supervisor, Chief Riding Officer Joshua Jeans, who unbelievably had also been a former mayor of Christchurch.

Jeans, who was obviously in league with John Streeter, the smuggling gang master, was found to have kept fraudulent records and allowed the smugglers a free passage for their contraband in return for a percentage of each consignment.

Leading up to the Battle of Mudeford, he had dismissed any suggestion that there was about to be a huge smuggling run and accordingly sent many customs officers home.

Both Bursey and Jeans were consequently dismissed from the Customs Service for their actions.

The customs officers had an unenviable and difficult job patrolling the coastline and they were supported in their endeavors by the army – namely the Dorset Yeomanry, whose commanding officer was Lewis Dymoke Grosvenor Tregonwell, a Dorset man from nearby Anderson.

In 1794, he established a barracks, in what is now Barrack Road, Christchurch (*see* Pre-war Aviation and the Second World War, Including Aviation and Aircraft Manufacture), from where his dragoons were also on hand to thwart a potential French invasion during the time of the Napoleonic Wars.

Did You Know?
In 1810, Tregonwell showed his wife the desolate sand dunes and heathland intersected by steep-sided ravines, known as 'chines', where he had patrolled in his search for smugglers. The Tregonwells fell in love with the area and bought $8^1/_2$ acres of land from the owner, George Tapps, on which they had a house built. They took up residence in 1812 and the remnants of these buildings still exist today as part of the Royal Exeter Hotel, Bournemouth. This was the first house in Bournemouth, meaning that Lewis Tregonwell is considered the founding father of the town.

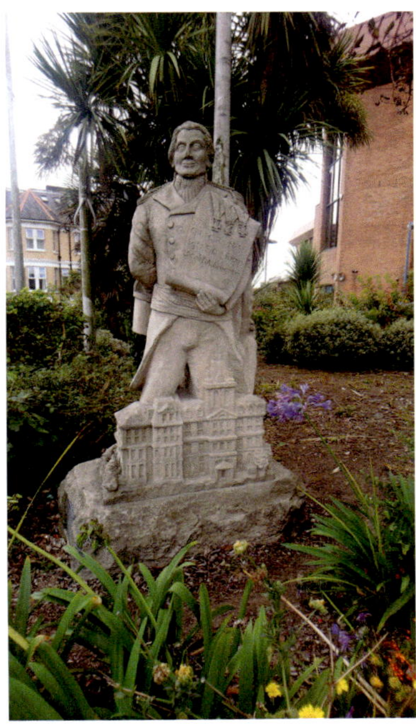

A statue of Lewis Dymoke Grosvenor Tregonwell situated outside the Bournemouth International Centre (BIC).

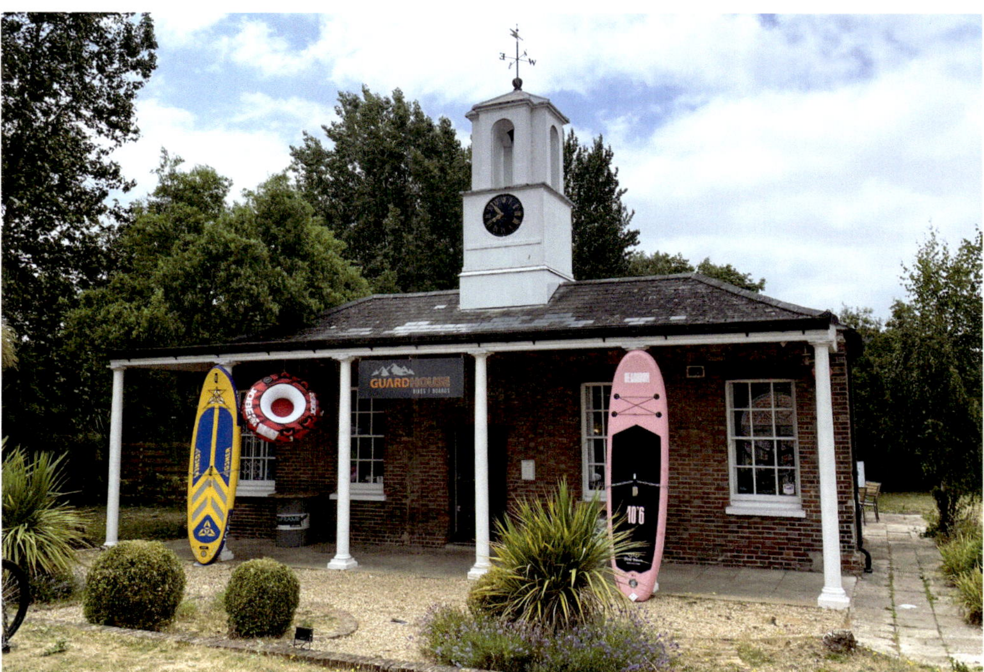

The Old Guard House.

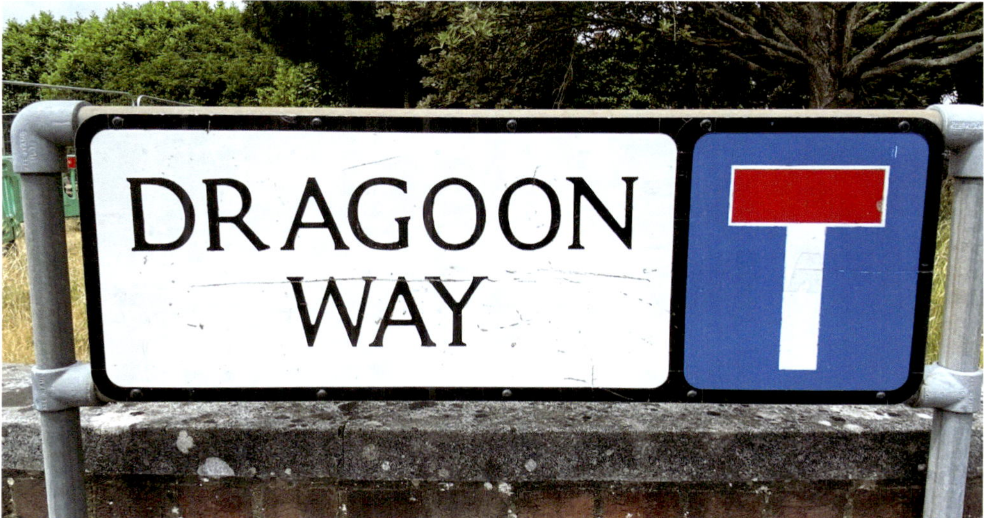

The former Military Experimental Establishment in Barrack Road had previously been a dragoon barracks, built in 1794 at the behest of Lewis Dymoke Grosvenor Tregonwell, the founder of Bournemouth and the commander of the Dorset Yeomanry (see Pre-War Aviation and the Second World War, Including Aviation and Aircraft Manufacture). The barracks later incorporated a guard house that was built in 1811. It is a Grade II listed building. The old barracks has been a housing estate since 1996, but the former guard house, stable block and officer's mess can still be seen.

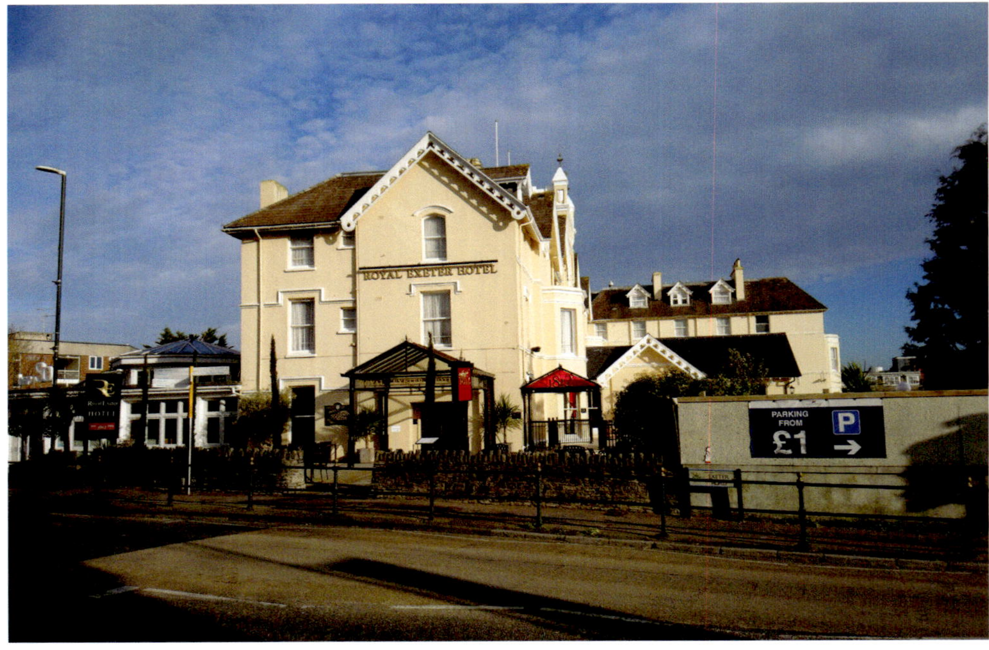

The Royal Exeter Hotel is at the site where the Tregonwells first made their home in Bournemouth. Some of the remnants of the original buildings still exist.

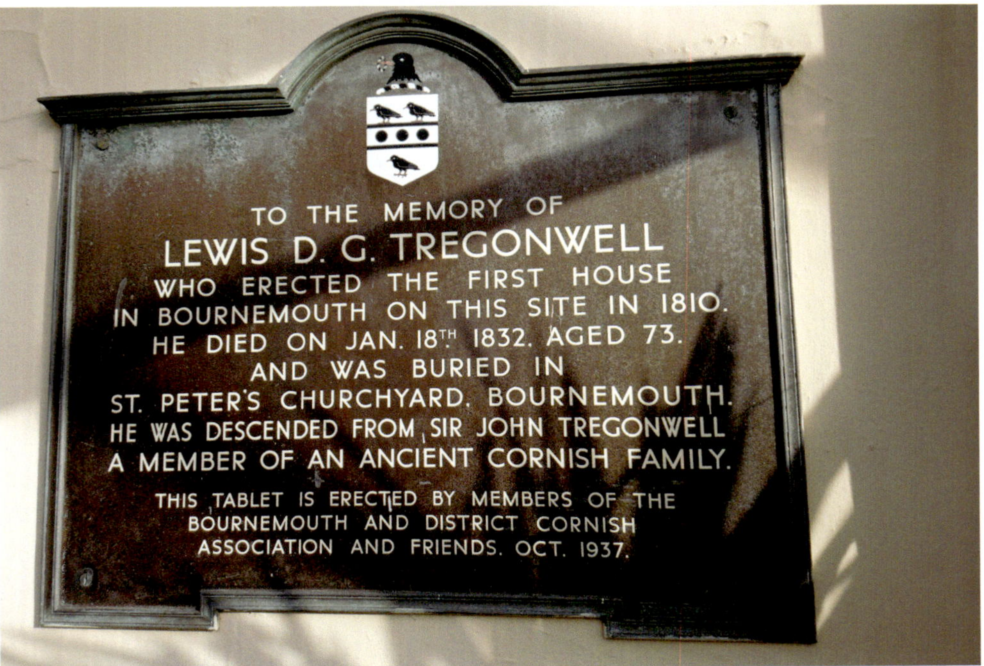

Plaque – Royal Exeter Hotel.

The investigations into the Battle of Mudeford and William Allen's murder also resulted in John Streeter, the local gang master and the owner of the smuggler's vessels, being sent to Winchester gaol. However, he subsequently managed to escape to the Channel Islands and later returned to Christchurch as part of an amnesty for smugglers introduced during the Napoleonic Wars. Upon his return, he was far from a reformed character and resumed his illegal activities with a vengeance, initiating a tobacco processing plant next door to the Ship in Distress public house. The tobacco business, although legitimate, was a front for all manner of nefarious activities, in which the landlady of the pub, Hannah Seller, who had taken over after she had been evicted from the Haven House Inn as a consequence of the Battle of Mudeford, was willingly complicit in storing much of his contraband.

The Ship in Distress was conveniently served by a channel across Stanpit Marsh, known as Mother Seller's Channel. It was navigable by small craft and ideal for bringing all manner of contraband right to the back door. The channel can still be seen today and is the one that the the Bailey Bridge prototype straddles (*see* Pre-war Aviation and the Second World War, Including Aviation and Aircraft Manufacture). However nowadays it is a shallower, narrower affair that stops well short of the pub.

Hannah Seller was also known as the 'Protecting Angel of Smugglers', or the 'Angel of the Marsh', and it was said that she would often turn out her customers to help smuggling ships in distress – hence the name of the pub. It is also claimed that one smuggler, Sam Hookey, chanced his arm navigating this route once too often and was drowned in the channel. He is now purported to haunt the pub and is reported to be the cause of strange unidentified noises.

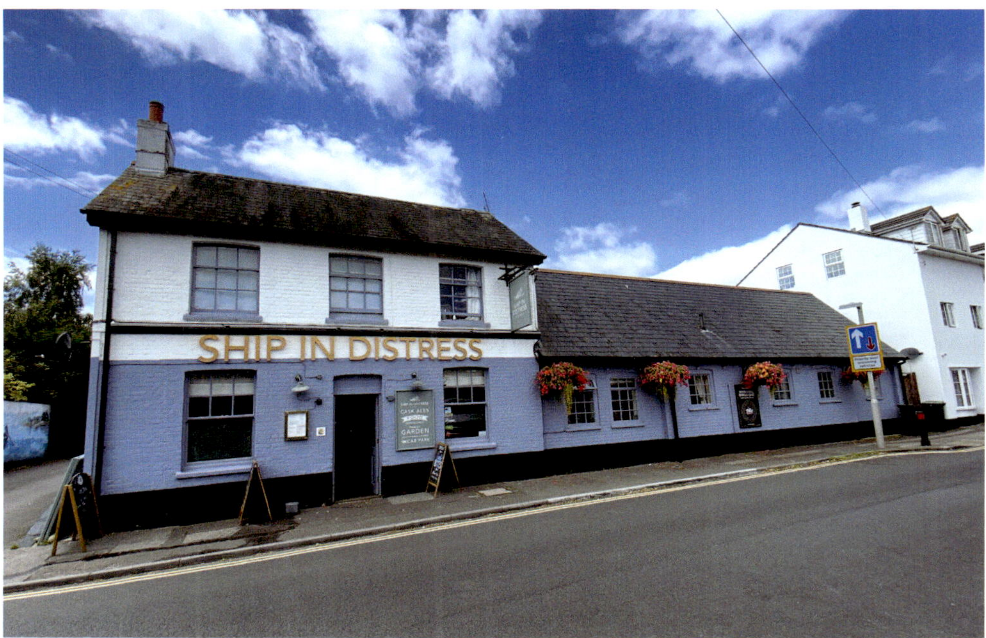

The Ship in Distress.

The Run at Mudeford Quay was closely patrolled after the Battle of Mudeford, but the illegal goods still continued to flow through virtually unabated, as the smugglers became ever more ingenious in getting the contraband into the Ship in Distress and elsewhere. This was despite coastguard cottages and a watchtower being installed overlooking Stanpit Marsh on the end of what is now Coastguard Way.

One smuggler, Abe Coates, had a unique way of getting contraband through. He was renowned for his supreme fitness and swimming ability, so was able to swim through the dangerous currents of the Run, hauling an underwater raft containing weighted tubs of spirit, which he then pulled into Mother Seller's Channel.

Meanwhile, John Streeter continued to receive vast amounts of contraband and was able to expand his business both legitimate, but mainly illegitimate, over a period of twenty years.

Another of the most prolific smugglers in the area was Isaac Gulliver (1745–1822), who, along with the army of people working for him, was responsible for a vast amount of illicit goods arriving from the sea. He was the son of a smuggler and inevitably he married into a smuggling family. He was Dorset's most celebrated and successful smuggler, although, he was actually born in Wiltshire.

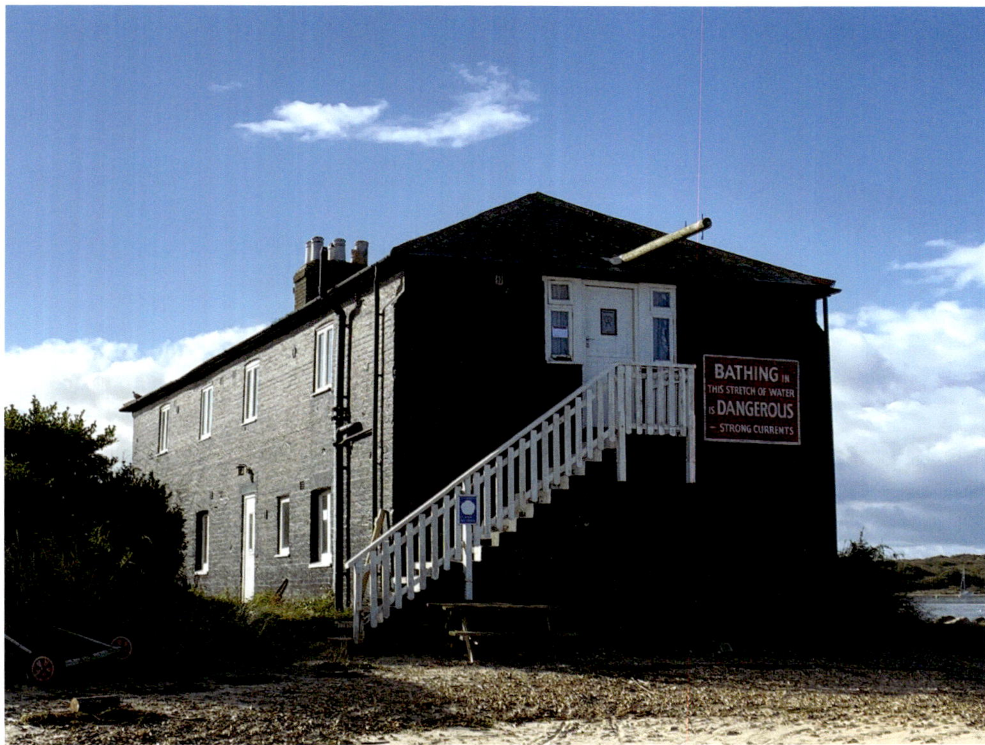

The Black House at the end of Mudeford Sandspit dates from the mid-seventeenth century and was used for shipbuilding. However, there are also accounts of the premises being used during a later period for storage of smuggled contraband.

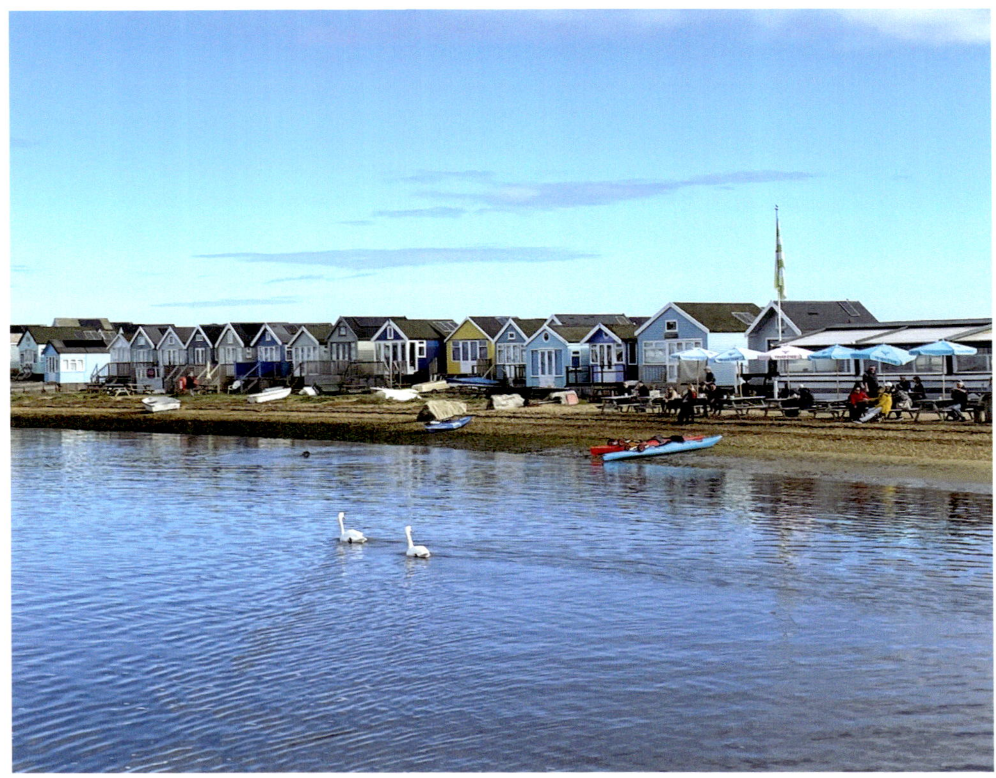

The Mudeford Sandspit is now lined with colourful beach huts.

In the late 1770s, he moved from Wiltshire to the White Hart Public House at Longham and then to West Howe House in Kinson, now in the Borough of Bournemouth, but in those days part of Poole. He controlled a massive smuggling operation which spread its tentacles across the whole of Dorset, Devon, Wiltshire and Hampshire. He even had the brass neck to provide his men with a kind of smuggling uniform which consisted of smocks and whitened hair – hence their nickname the 'White Wigs'.

He became a wanted man after his involvement in a clash with customs officers between Bournemouth and Poole. However, he regularly evaded their attention, and on one occasion was secreted out of the King's Head in Poole, hidden inside a barrel, under the very noses of customs officials. On another occasion, he eluded customs men by lying motionless in a coffin with his face covered with white powder as he played dead.

Of course, it didn't go unnoticed to Gulliver that Christchurch was an ideal location for his activities. He had a fleet of fifteen luggers, from which his men would unload the contraband on the coastline. What couldn't be transported was immediately concealed. The rest was transported with the aid of packhorses to holding areas via heathland from the coast to the Stour valley and beyond through Hurn and West Parley to Wimborne and Cranborne as well as through the Avon valley. It was then distributed by his fleet of horse-drawn wagons as far afield as the Midlands, London, Bristol and Bath.

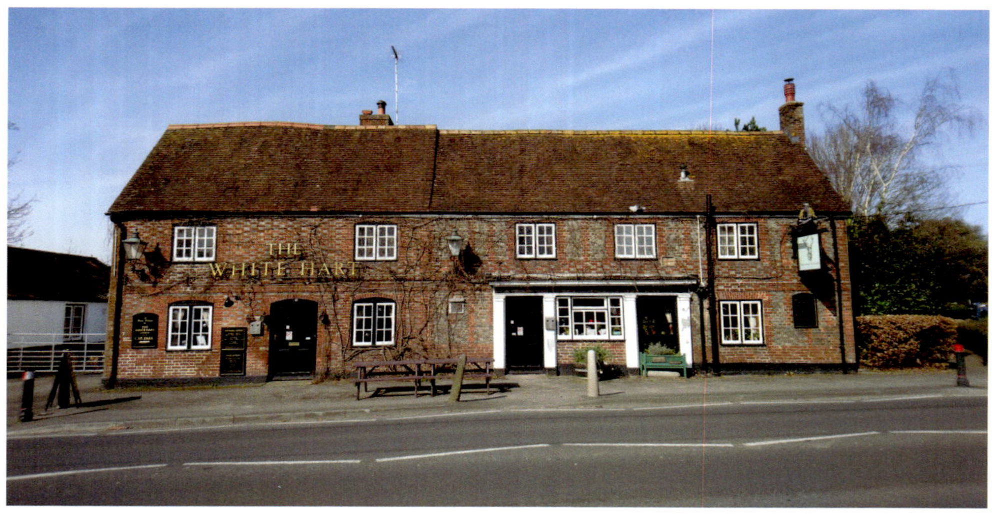

The White Hart, Longham.

Having amassed a tidy fortune, Gulliver eventually retired from smuggling and was given a King's Pardon by George III (r. 1760–1820). This was believed to have been, because he discovered a plot to assassinate the monarch, and alerted the authorities. A grateful George III is supposed to have said, 'Let Gulliver smuggle as much as he wants,' which may explain how he was never caught and was able to smuggle with impunity

He then became a wine merchant (although it was believed that a large proportion of his wine was of the smuggled variety), banker, civic leader and churchwarden in Wimborne. Upon his death, he was buried in the vault of Wimborne Minster. His legacy still lives on throughout Dorset, but despite his powerful build, he was considered to have been a gentleman, who never used the pistol, which now resides in the Russell Cotes Museum, Bournemouth.

After arrival by sea at Christchurch, much of the contraband was transported through the New Forest into the hands of the Warne family, a disreputable smuggling family who lived at a house called Knave's Ash at Crow Hill Top, near Burley. The two brothers, John and Peter, ran goods from Christchurch and Lymington, assisted by their sister, Lovey.

Many tales have been associated with Lovey Warne and she was renowned for parading around in a red cloak across Vereley Hill in the New Forest to signify to her brothers that the revenue men were around.

She also played a more hands-on role, which often involved visiting smuggling ships at Christchurch and unchanging in the privacy of the captain's cabin, before wrapping numerous valuable silks around her person and then putting her clothes back on over the top. She must have looked considerably fatter after this procedure but the revenue men never seemed to notice. However, on one occasion she was nearly discovered when a revenue man started getting amorous with her in the Eight Bells public house and began to move his hands up her thighs perilously close to the hidden silks. However, Lovey managed to refute his advances and the silks remained undiscovered.

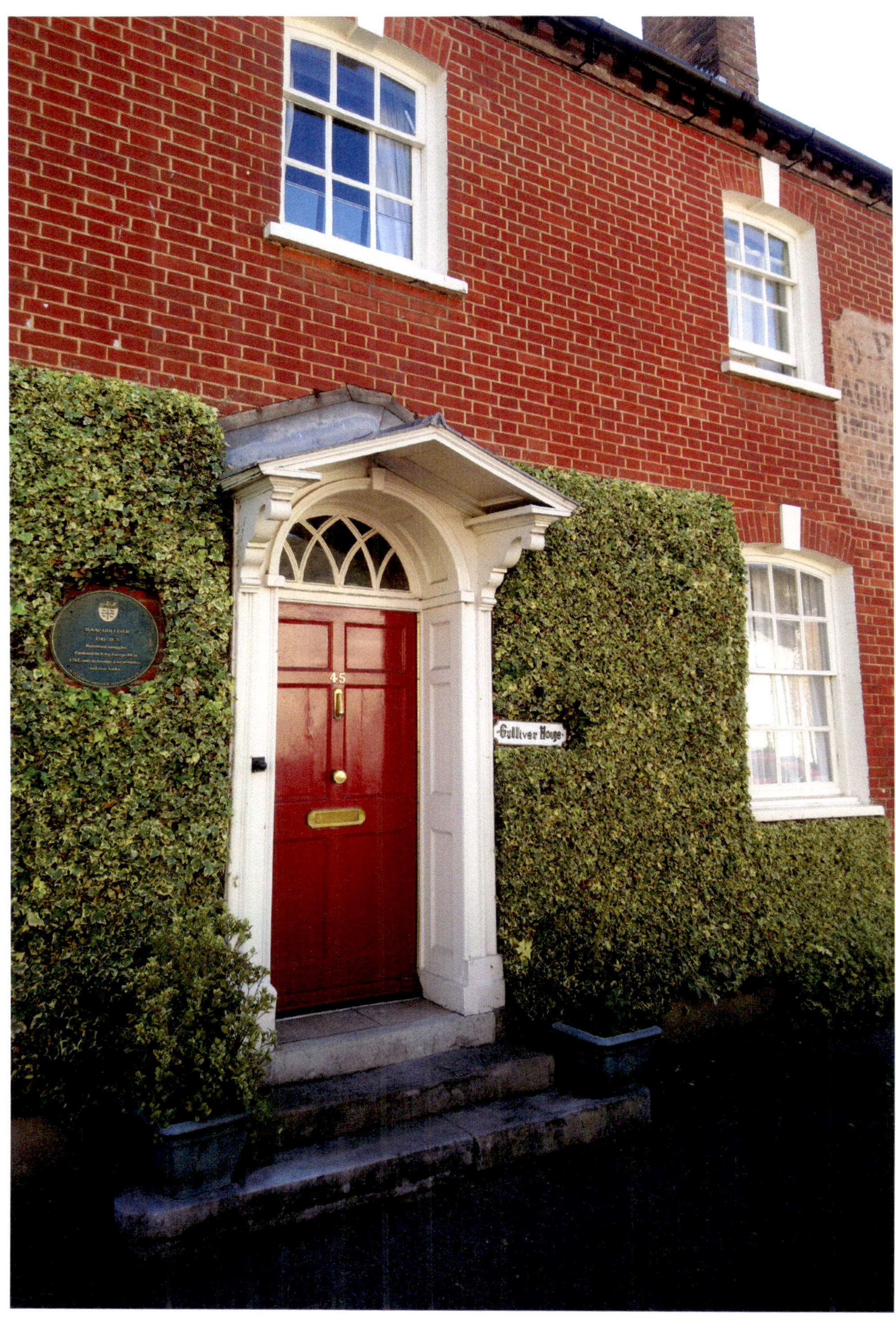

Gulliver's House, Wimborne.

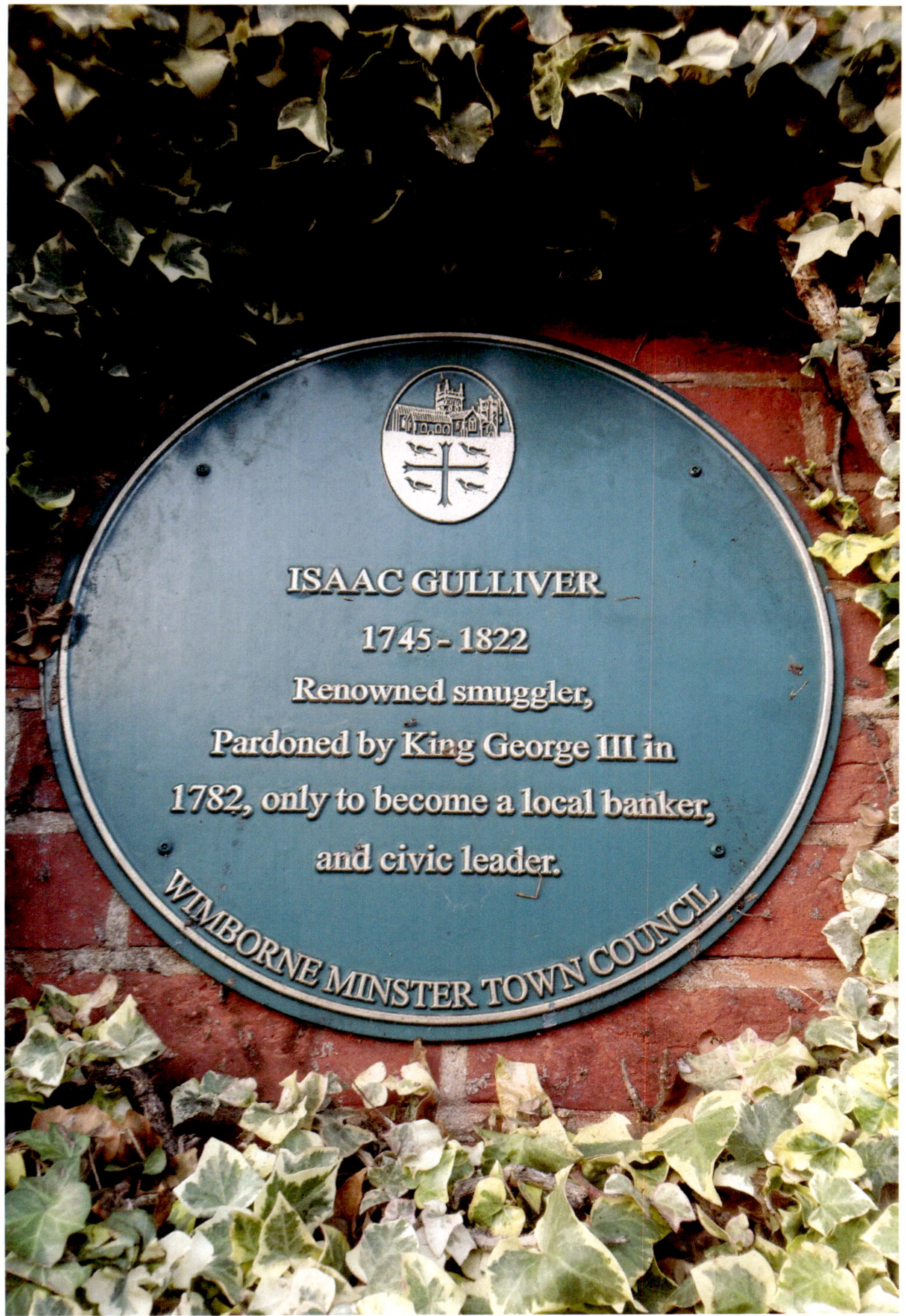

Plaque – Gulliver's House.

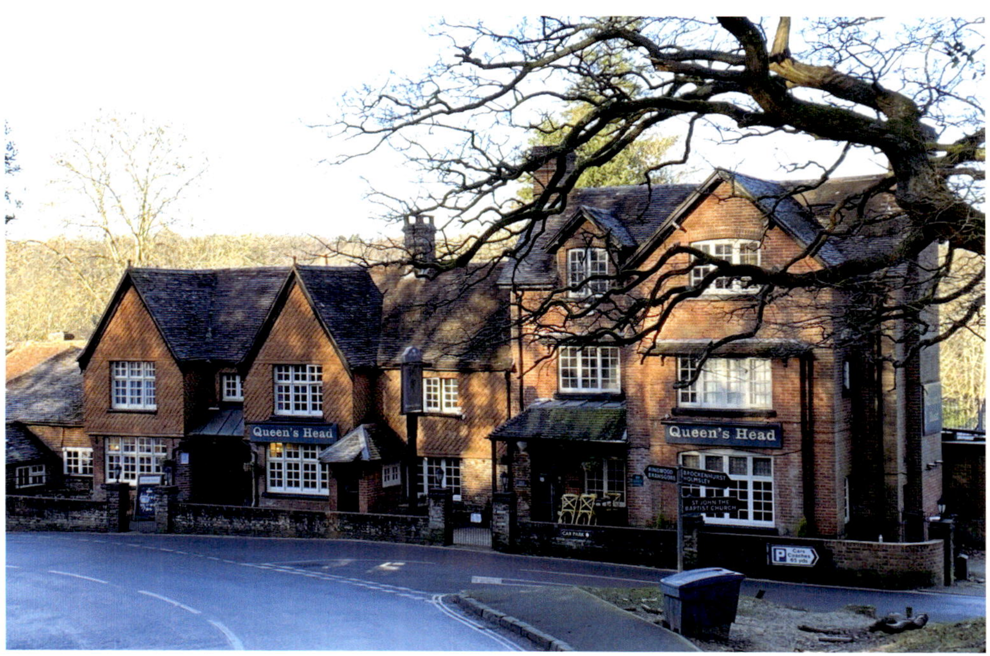

The Warne family are commemorated for posterity at Warne's Bar at the Queen's Head Inn, Burley. Secret cellars were discovered at the pub during building work.

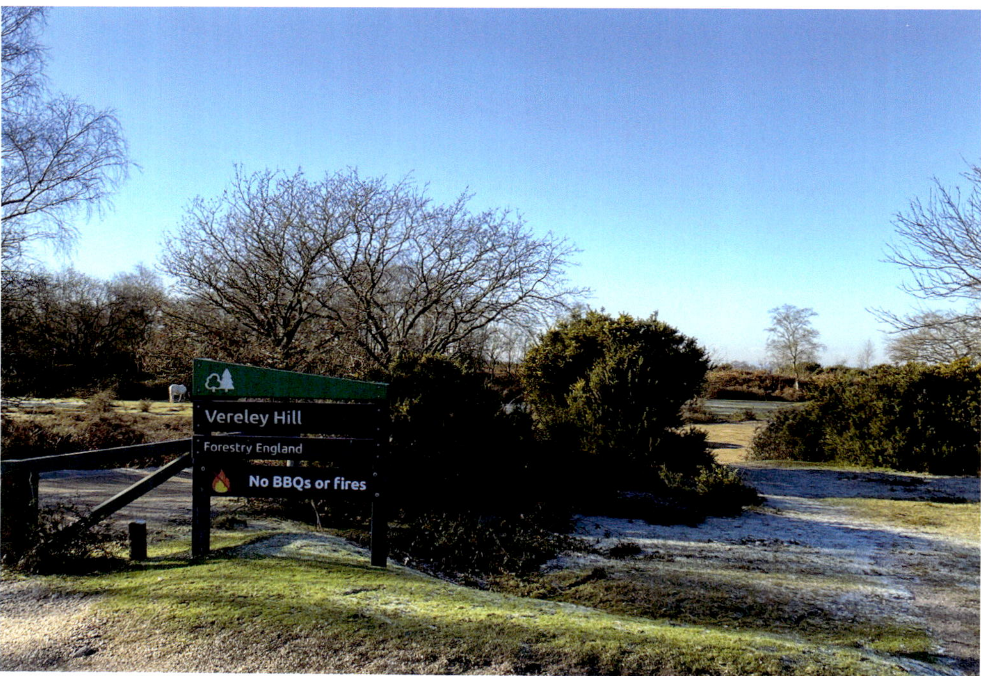

Vereley Hill where Lovey wore her red cloak.

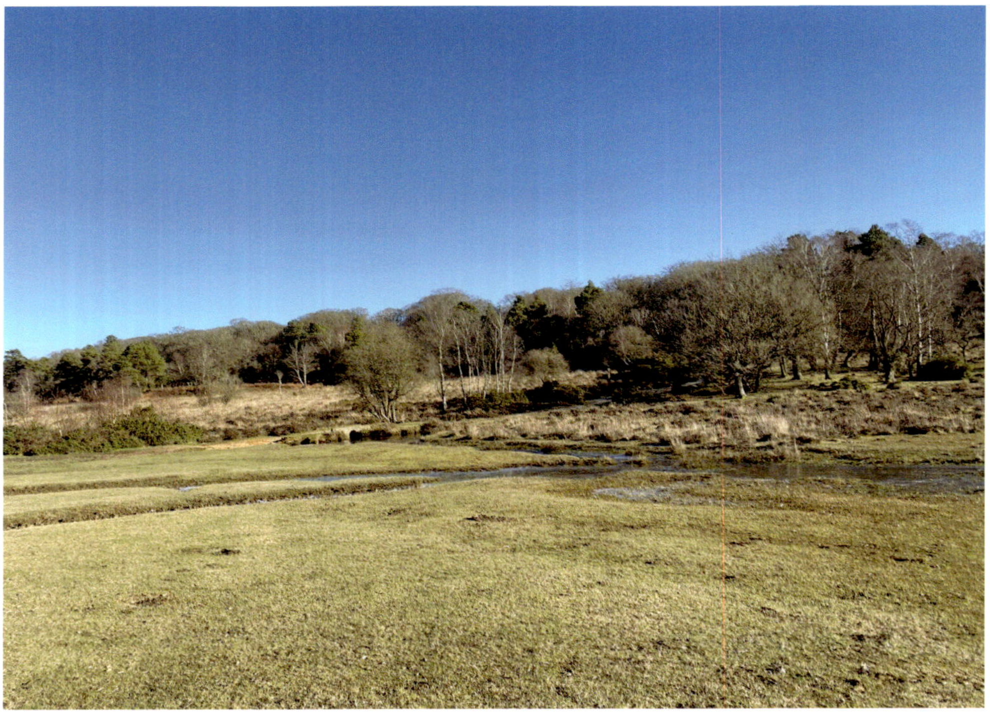

Near Vereley Hill is Ridley Wood, which served as a smuggler's market place. This image shows a ford at Ridley Bottom at the edge of the wood.

The Eight Bells was yet another smuggling den of inequity within the town and was said to have had tunnels leading to the priory. According to local legend, revenue officers searched the inn one day for hidden contraband, but were unable to find anything, mainly because the landlord's wife, Kate Preston, was concealing the brandy tubs in question under her voluminous petticoats.

The smuggling heritage of Christchurch is reflected in many of the pubs, and certainly this is true of Christchurch's oldest pub, Ye Olde George Inn. This Grade II listed coaching inn was first called the St George in 1630 and then later the George and Dragon, before changing to its current name. It still retains the stone floor and the atmospheric low beams of the original timbered building.

Did You Know?
A coach from Lymington called the Emerald Coach regularly stopped at Ye Olde George Inn to pick up felons temporarily incarcerated within prison cells at the pub before taking them onwards to Poole for transportation to the Australian continent. The remnants of the prison cell can still be seen today.

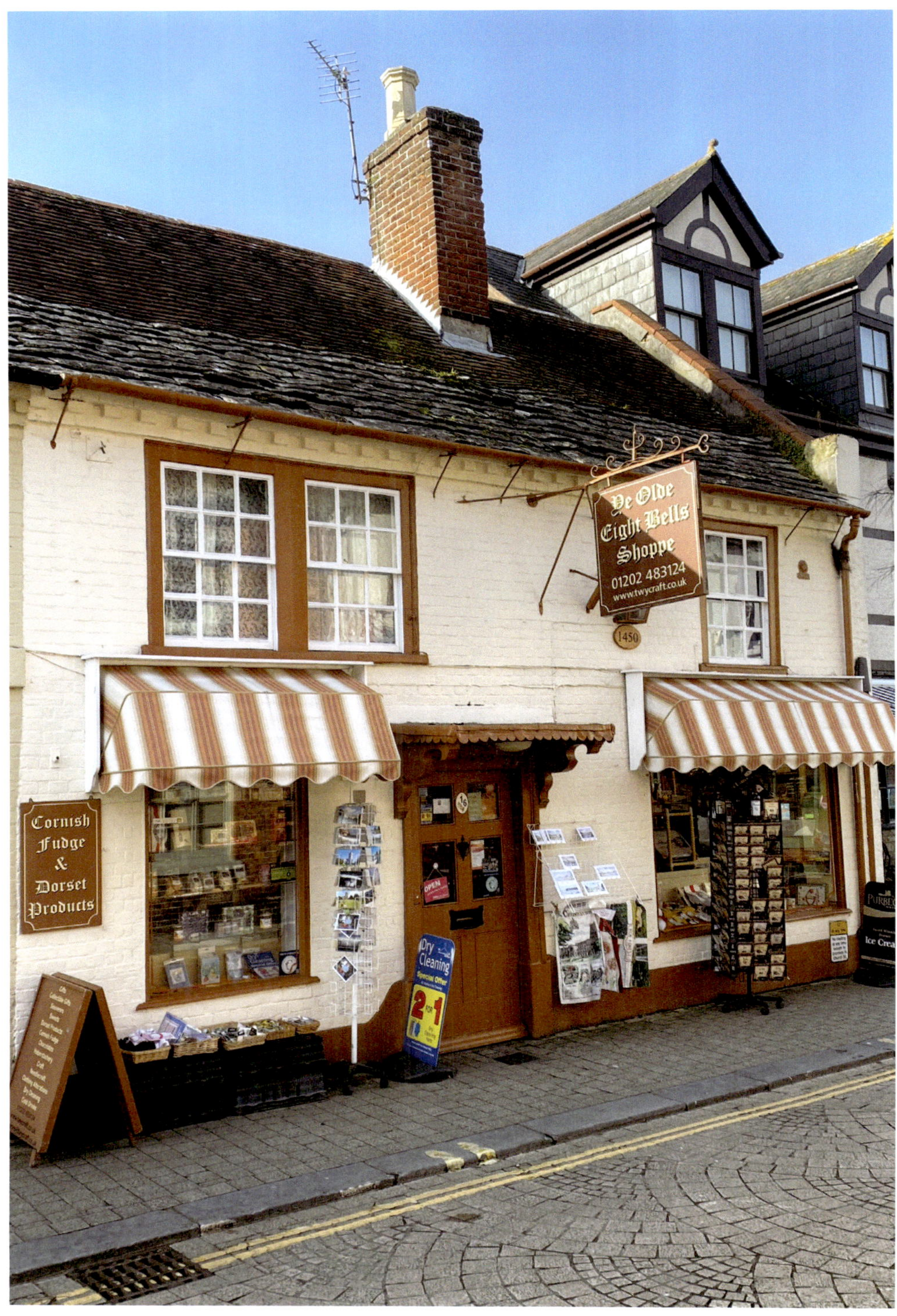

The former Eight Bells pub in Church Street was once a smugglers' haunt, but is now a gift shop.

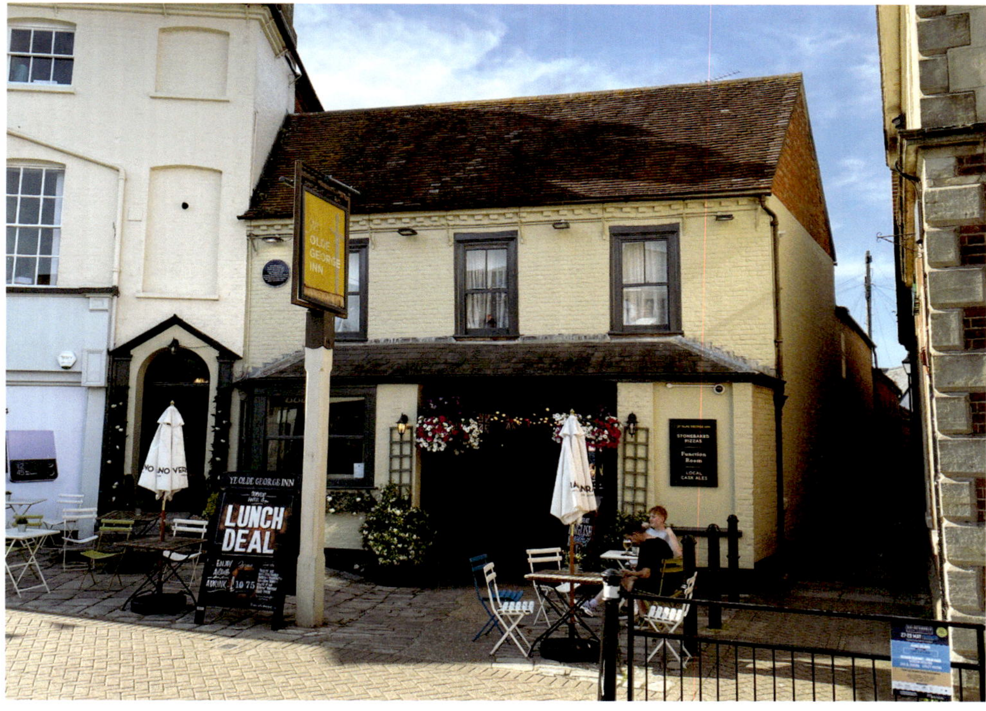

Ye Olde George Inn.

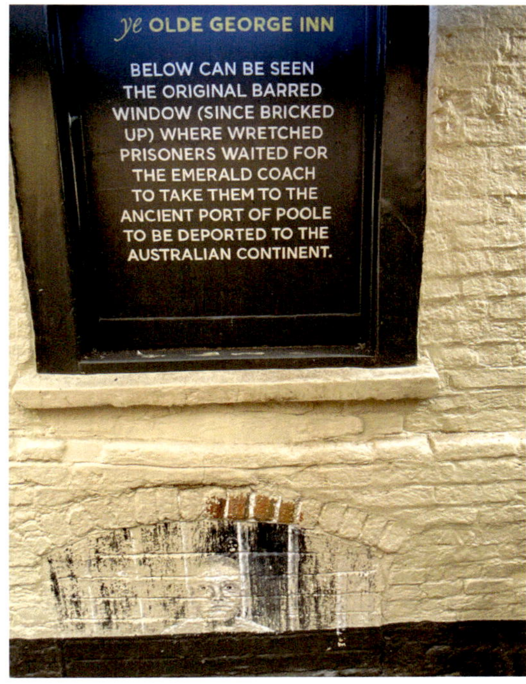

The prison cell at Ye Olde George Inn.

It seems that the majority of the pub's clientele tended to be from the smuggling fraternity, despite the somewhat off-putting proximity of the prison cells. It is also rumoured that like the Eight Bells, there were tunnels underneath the George leading to Christchurch Priory, for additional storage of illicit goods.

Until recently there were various smuggling artifacts dotted around the pub including several barrels that were used to 'seed the sea'. This was a system used by smugglers on the occasions that they were under severe pressure to unload their illicit cargo, due to the proximity of customs officers. In these instances they wouldn't unload the goods on the shore and instead would tie ropes to the barrels before throwing them overboard. The ropes had an iron bar at one end to ensure they stayed submerged and a cork attached to the other, to enable the crew of a smuggling cutter to identify and retrieve the contraband at a later date.

A well-respected doctor by the name of Arthur Quarterley lived near to Ye Olde George Inn and there is a monument in the priory in his honour. The inscription reads 'sacred to the memory of Arthur Quarterley Esq M.D. The last line of the inscription reads 'highly respected and deeply lamented by all classes of society'.

On one occasion he was rudely awakened in the dead of night by some smugglers who took him to a cottage in Bransgore in the New Forest, where he encountered a member of the smuggling gang lying on a bed, having been severely wounded from a musket shot to his shoulder. The doctor removed the offending musket ball, before giving instructions that the man should rest and not be moved. However, the wounded smuggler was having none of it and piped up that he would prefer to be moved rather than finish his days on the end of a rope. Accordingly, his gang moved him to a safe house in the New Forest where he made a full recovery. Later, Dr Quarterley was duly rewarded for his efforts when several kegs of brandy turned up on his doorstep with a note attatched saying, 'Left here for the doctor's fee'.

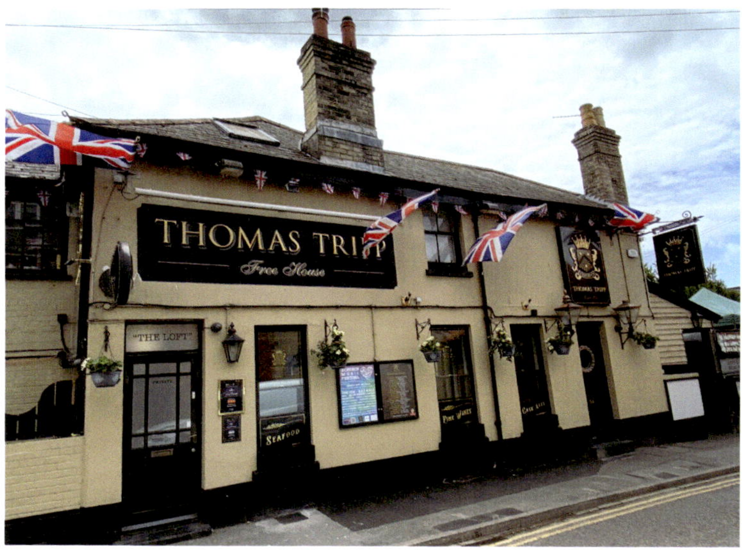

The Thomas Tripp.

The Thomas Tripp, which dates back to 1750, is also known for its smuggling connections and like many Christchurch pubs around this time, the majority of the regulars were smugglers, including a certain Mr Thomas Tripp, who reputedly had his last pint in this pub before he was arrested and later hanged at Tower Hill in London.

The Ship is another old pub with smuggling connections. It dates from the fifteenth century and still possesses the low ceilings and timber beams of this period.

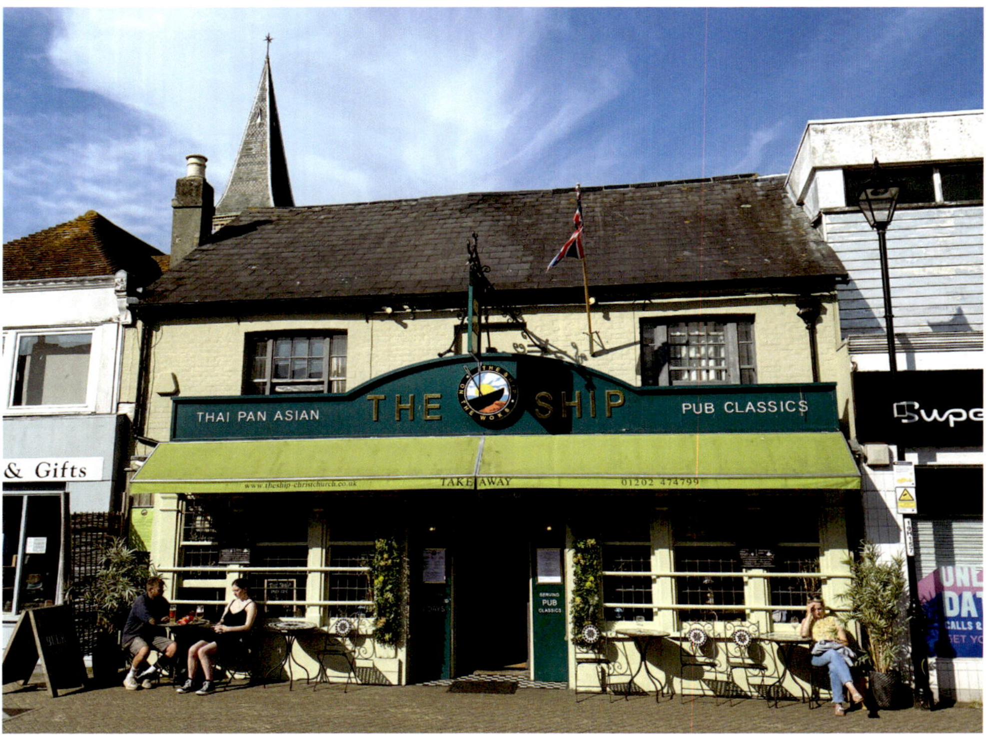

The Ship.

4. Pre-war Aviation and the Second World War, Including Aviation and Aircraft Manufacture

Christchurch played a significant role in contributing to the golden age of British aviation between the 1940s and 1970s. However, there are very few reminders of this now apart from some street names such as Rolls Drive, Halifax Way, Valiant Way, Brabazon Drive, Ambassador Close, Dakota Close, Airspeed Way, Airfield Way and the Runway.

Christchurch's earliest involvement with the aviation industry resulted in the unfortunate demise of one half of Rolls-Royce.

Charles Rolls (1877–1910) was one of the leading lights in the world of motoring and it was through the Royal Automobile Club that he met his business partner, Henry Royce, in 1904. However, Rolls' overriding passion was for aviation in all its forms, and in 1909 he purchased one of six Wright Brothers aircraft and became only the second Englishman to go up in an aeroplane. He then went on to make more than 200 flights, and became the first man to make a double crossing of the English Channel by plane on 2 June 1910. He was also an experienced balloonist who made over 170 assents.

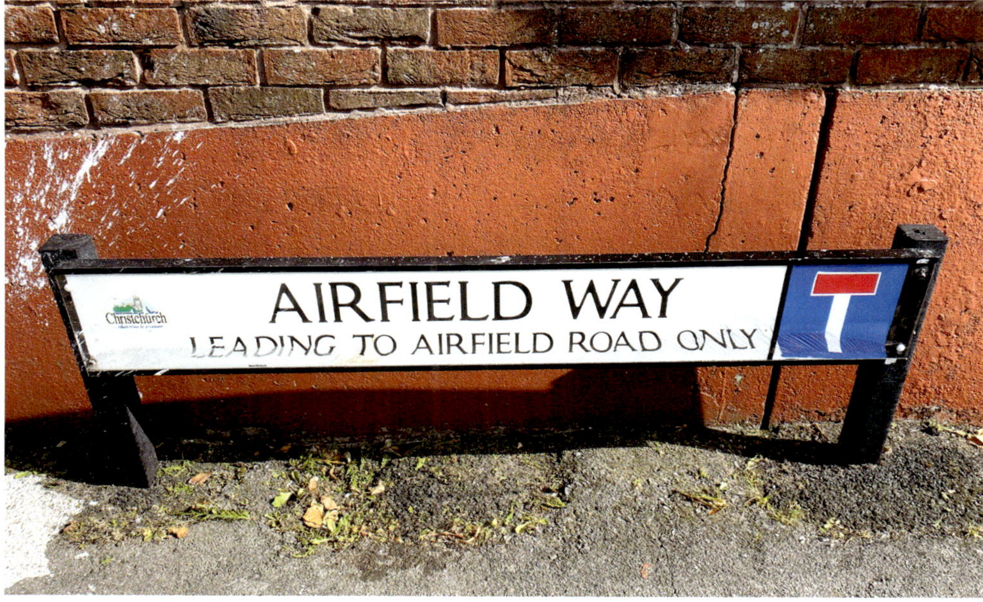

Airfield Way.

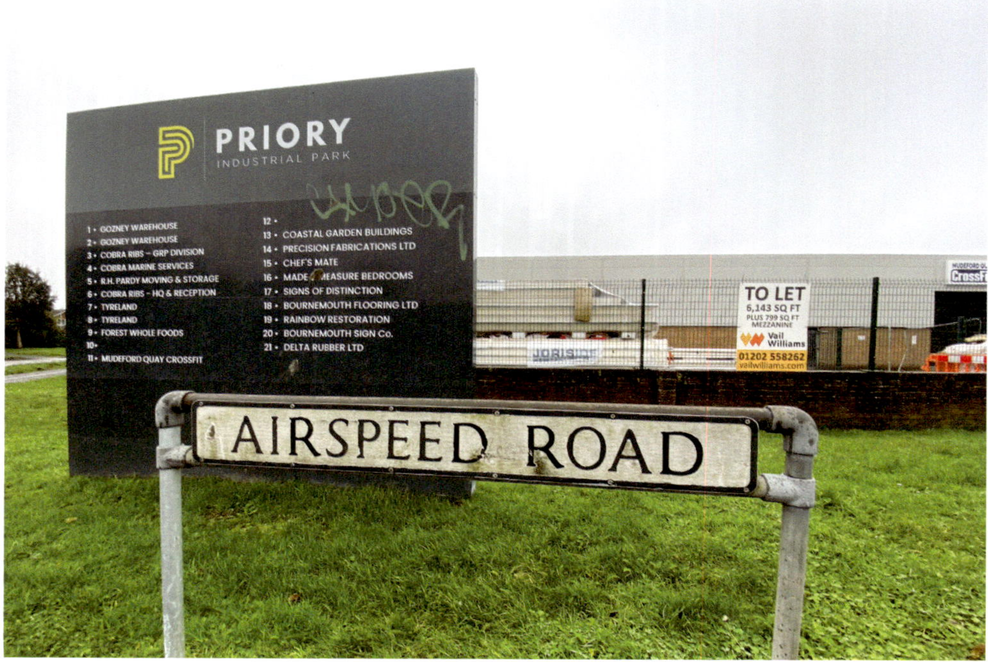

Airspeed Road.

He later came to an agreement with Henry Royce, enabling him to step back from his day-to-day involvement with the firm, so that he could focus on flying. Shortly afterwards on 12 July 1910, he took part in Britain's first international aviation meeting at Hengistbury Airfield, which formed part of Bournemouth's Centenary celebrations.

Flying his Wright Brothers bi-plane, he attempted a pin-point landing on a marked spot. However, the tail snapped and the plane suddenly plummeted to earth. He was thrown from the aircraft and killed instantly on impact. A plaque in the playing field of St Peter's School, which was unveiled in 1981, marks the spot of the crash with the words: 'This stone commemorates the Hon Charles Stewart Rolls who was killed in a flying accident near this spot on 12 July 1910; the first Briton to die in a powered flight.'

Sixteen years later aviation had become a little more established and again the Christchurch area was very much in the vanguard. An organisation called Surrey Flying Services started offering pleasure flights from a field known as Barry's Field within Mudeford Farm, and then later from fields close to Somerford Road.

In 1930, Francis Fisher started Fisher Aviation Company in fields that he rented towards the eastern end of Somerford Road and business flourished to such an extent that in the following year he sought permission to build an aerodrome. However, he had some difficulties with this, as these new-fangled flying machines were not to everyone's taste and plenty of opposition to the airfield was lodged, mainly due to the noise and the disruption that had been caused to services at the priory by Alan Cobham's Flying Circus the previous year.

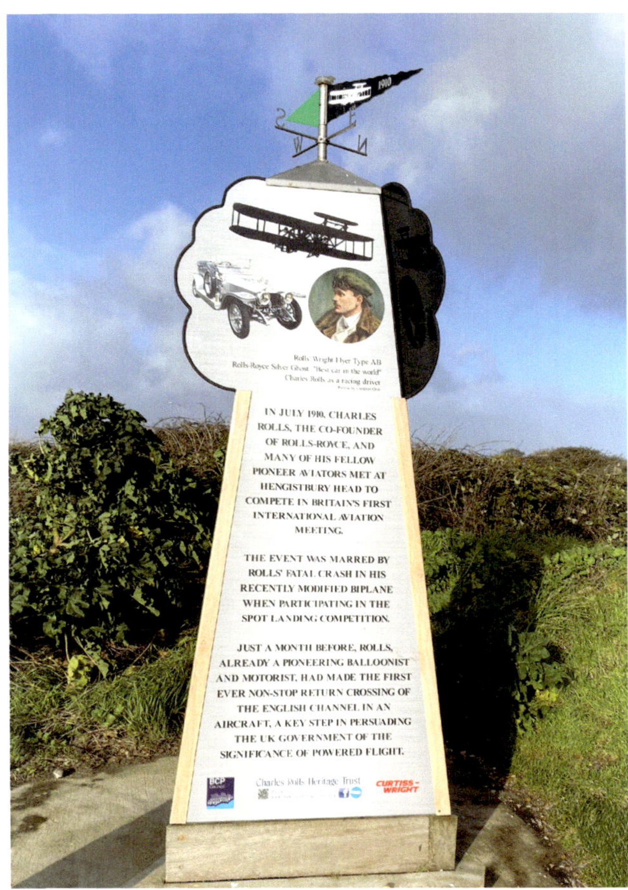

Charles Rolls Memorial.

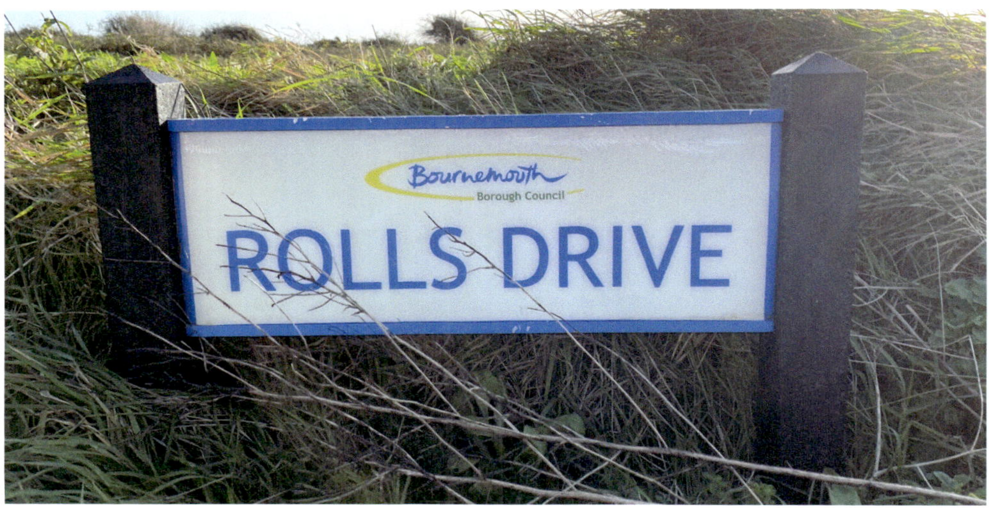

Rolls Drive.

However, despite the initial objections from the town's worthy burghers, planning application was granted after an appeal and the site become known as Christchurch Airfield. It was bordered by Mudeford Lane, Stroud Lane and Bure Lane. Meanwhile, Alan Cobham went on to establish himself as an aviation pioneer and set up the local firm Flight Refuelling, which was later to become Cobham Aviation Services.

In 1936, Christchurch was the scene of a spectacular crash involving a Miles Satyr wooden bi-plane built by George Parnell and Company.

Mrs Victor Bruce, the pilot and owner of the plane, was giving a display in aid of charity. She wasn't unduly worried to see a cluster of telephone wires as she approached the landing site as she assumed she would just go right through them. However, the combination of the number of wires and the low speed of the plane resulted in the plane being catapulted backwards. Luckily she survived the crash.

A more auspicious event occurred at Christchurch in 1937 when Jean Batten landed, having flown from Australia on a solo flight that was completed in a record time of five days, eighteen hours and fifteen minutes.

Two years later, Britain was at war and in the early days of the conflict, like the rest of Britain, Christchurch was anticipating a possible invasion and accordingly, Christchurch Airfield was protected by a number of pill boxes. The environs of the town were also heavily fortified with pill boxes, gun emplacements and tank traps, while the approach roads to the beaches were barricaded with anti-tank devices. The beaches themselves were also mined and surrounded with barbed wire.

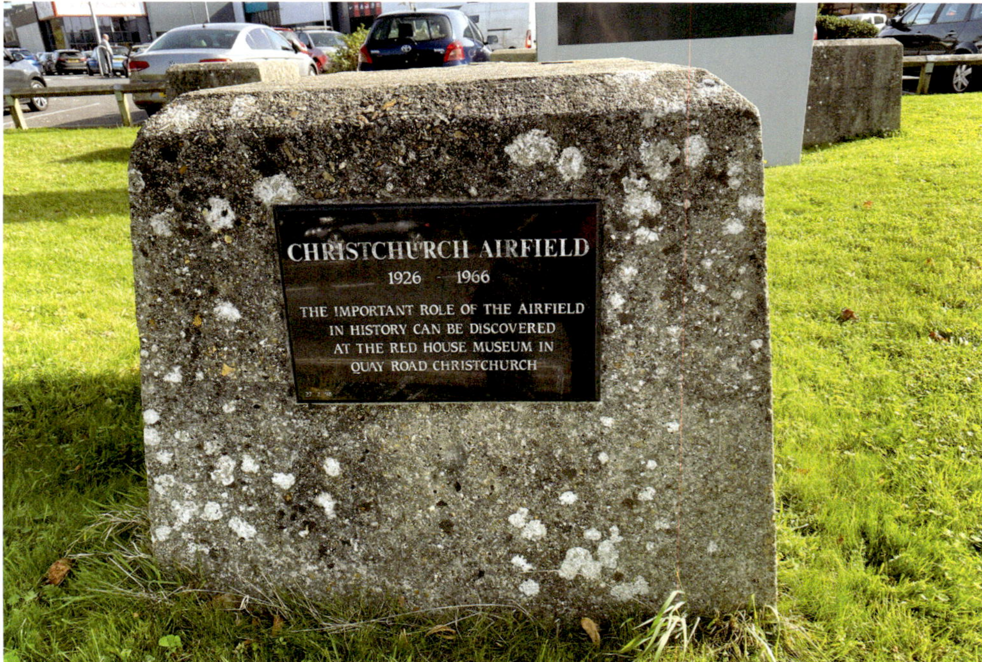

Plaque – Christchurch Airfield.

It was thought that if Christchurch could hold out against the German 6th Army potentially arriving from Cherbourg, that this would prevent them from linking up with other invading German factions; so consequently, the area between the two rivers to the north of the town was also guarded by a line of tank traps.

Pill Boxes were built throughout Britain, as a defence against a possible invasion between 1940 and 1941. One was built on an island near the Town Bridge which covered the Avon, whereas the Stour was covered by a pill box near Tuckton Bridge. Further pill boxes were positioned at the end of Mudeford Quay and a much larger one occupied what is now Sandhills Holiday Park, overlooking Avon Beach. Pill boxes were also situated in Ringwood Road and at Roeshot Hill. The Home Guard manned a pill box to the north of the town as well as manning Highcliffe Castle, where it has been suggested anecdotally that some of the paths in the vicinity still contain pipe mines. However, a UXO (Unexploded Ordnance) assessment failed to find any in 2017.

Stanpit Marsh was utilised by the military in both World Wars as a testing ground for military engineering. One such example is the Bailey Bridge and a mock-up of the original prototype that was situated here can be observed crossing a tributary called Mother Seller's Channel (*see* Smuggling).

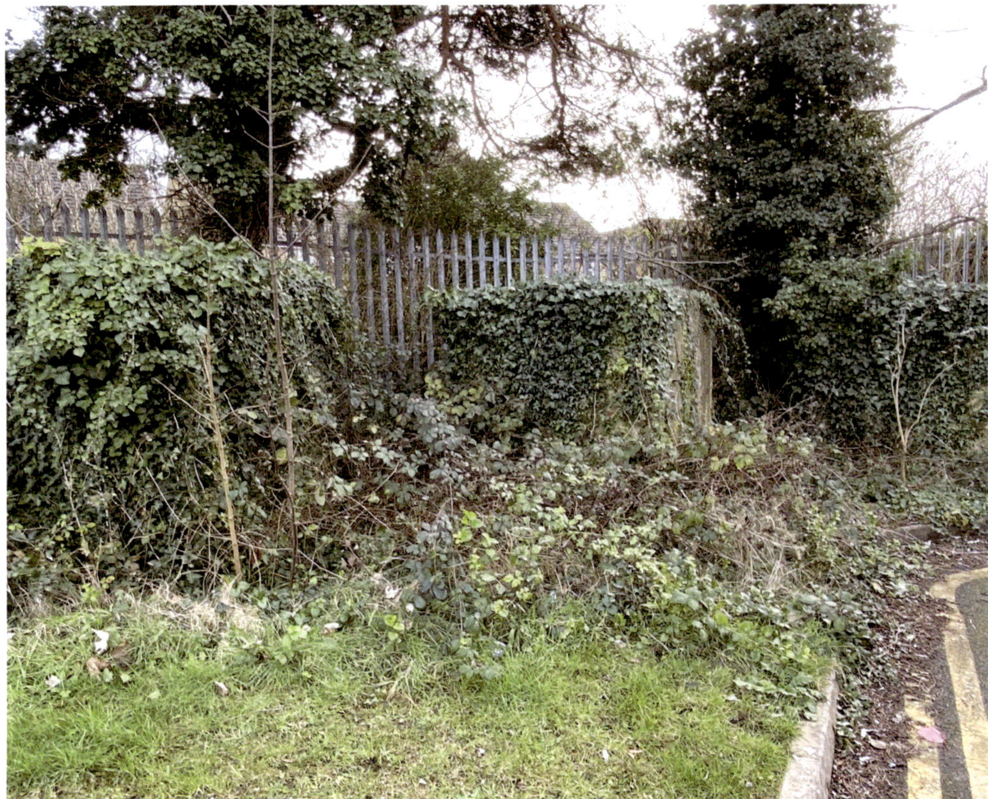

Part of the line of Tank Traps – somewhat overgrown now.

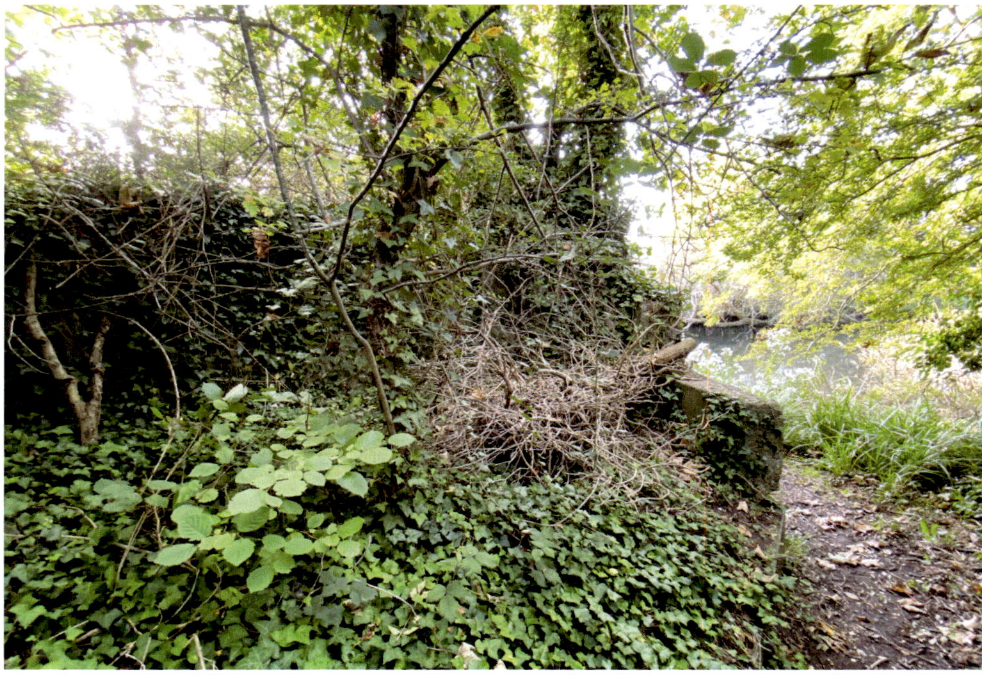

Tuckton Bridge Pill Box – also somewhat overgrown.

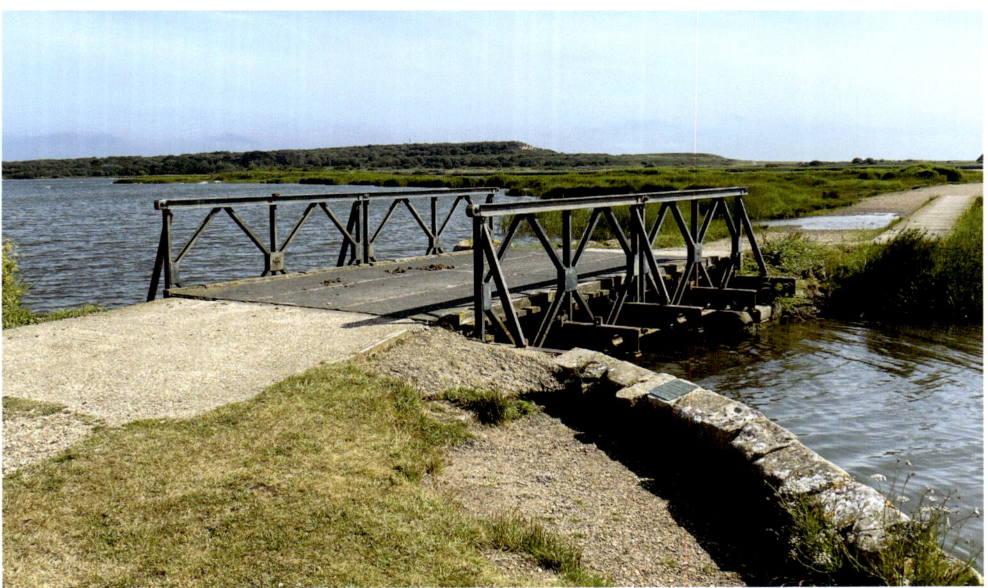

Bailey Bridge, Stanpit Marsh. This innocuous bridge may not look much but it played a pivotal part in winning the Second World War. The present bridge was donated by the Royal Armament Research and Development Establishment, Christchurch, in 1984 to replace the original prototype that was previously situated here.

The former Military Experimental Establishment in Barrack Road had previously been a dragoon barracks, built in 1794 at the behest of Lewis Dymoke Grosvenor Tregonwell (*see* Smuggling). In 1918, the Royal Engineers moved into the barracks, including a section called the Bridge Company which changed its name in 1925 to the Experimental Bridging Establishment (EBE). Their role was to develop portable bridges that would enable tanks to cross rivers.

Civilians were also employed at this establishment, including a certain Mr Donald Bailey, who started there in 1928 and worked there throughout the Second World War. His department had been involved in trials of the Inglis Bridge, which were not proving very successful. After one such unsuccessful trial, he was returning to Christchurch with his colleague, Major S. A. Steward, when Bailey pulled out a piece of paper from his back pocket of a bridge he had secretly been working on himself. Steward was very impressed and authorised further investigation to start immediately.

A factory making the components for the bridge was established at the Experimental Bridging Establishment. The dedicated design team was overseen by Bailey and they worked many long hours to get the bridge operationally ready very quickly. The bridge was made of pre-fabricated sections, which gave it the advantage of being light and relatively easy to carry for military personnel. They were simple and quick to construct and were instrumental in allowing Allied forces to move tanks across rivers and make speedy progress through Europe after the D-Day landings.

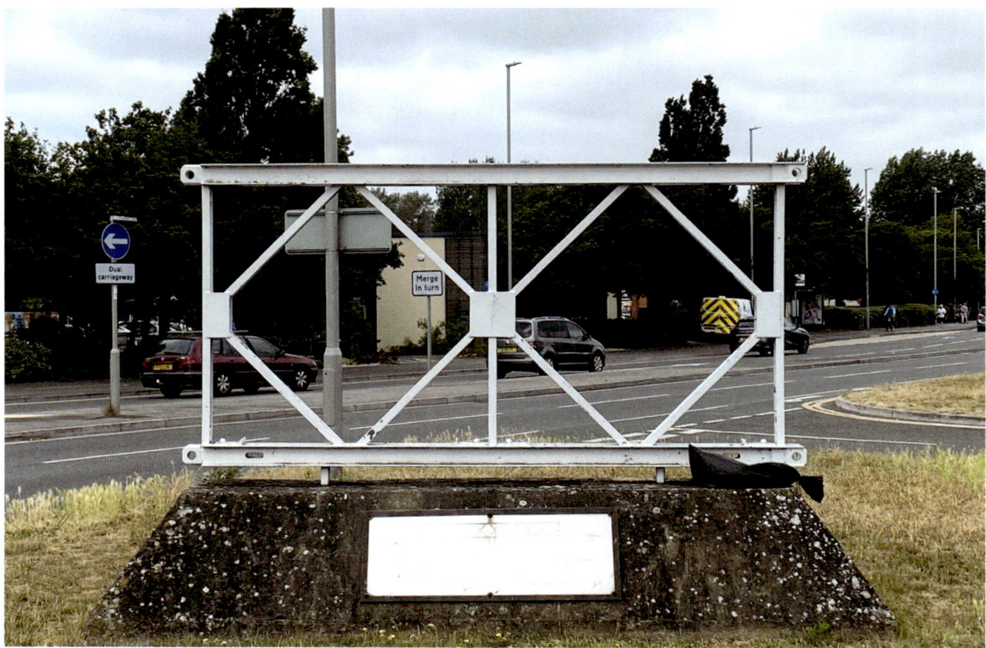

A Bailey Bridge section now stands on a roundabout opposite where the former Military Experimental Establishment at Christchurch was and where the iconic Bailey Bridge was conceived and manufactured.

Did You Know?
Donald Bailey was awarded the OBE in 1943 and was knighted in 1946. Field Marshal Montgomery praised the contribution the Bailey Bridge made in winning the war and Eisenhower was similarly impressed, describing the bridge as one of the three most important engineering and technological inventions of the Second World War, along with radar and the heavy bomber.

Bailey later became director of MEXE (Military Engineering Experimental Establishment), which the former Experimental Bridging Establishment at Christchurch became, and then was the Dean of the Royal Military College at Shrivenham, Oxfordshire, before returning to live in Christchurch until his death in 1985.

Another relic of the war that can be found on Stanpit Marsh is a rusting hull of a former lifeboat that once served as a lifeboat on a US *Liberty* ship. These were cargo ships, which were a British concept but built in America under the Emergency Shipping Programme. They were of a low-cost design and were mass produced in great volumes, ostensibly to replace British cargo ships that were being destroyed in vast numbers by German U-boats.

After the war, she was used as a lifeboat locally, before coming to grief during a storm in 1953, resulting in her being swept across Priory Marsh to where she now stands.

Sadly the details of the *Liberty* ship the vessel was once attatched to are unknown.

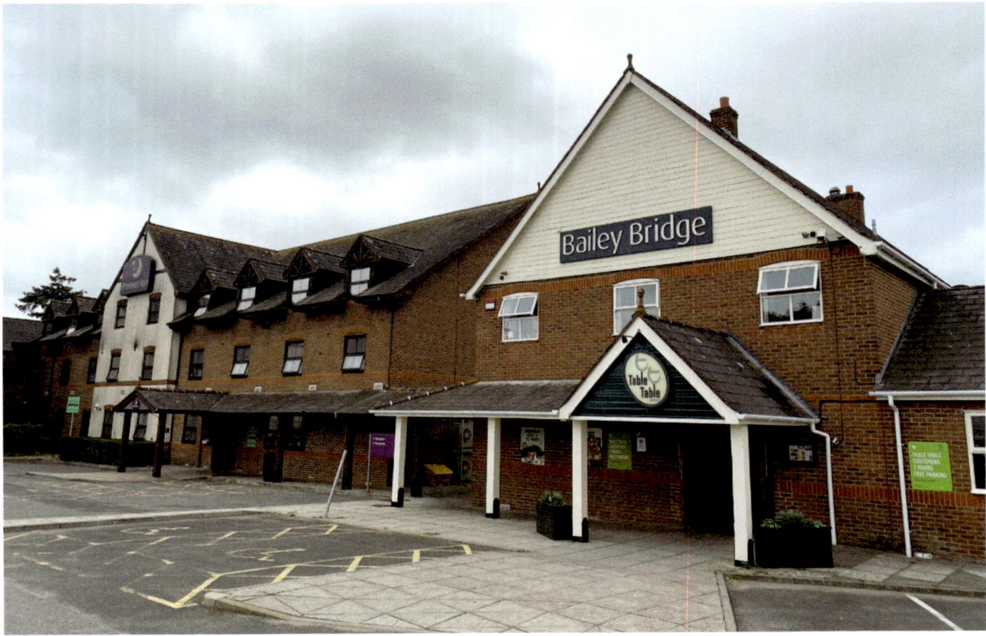

The suitably named Bailey Bridge pub is nearby.

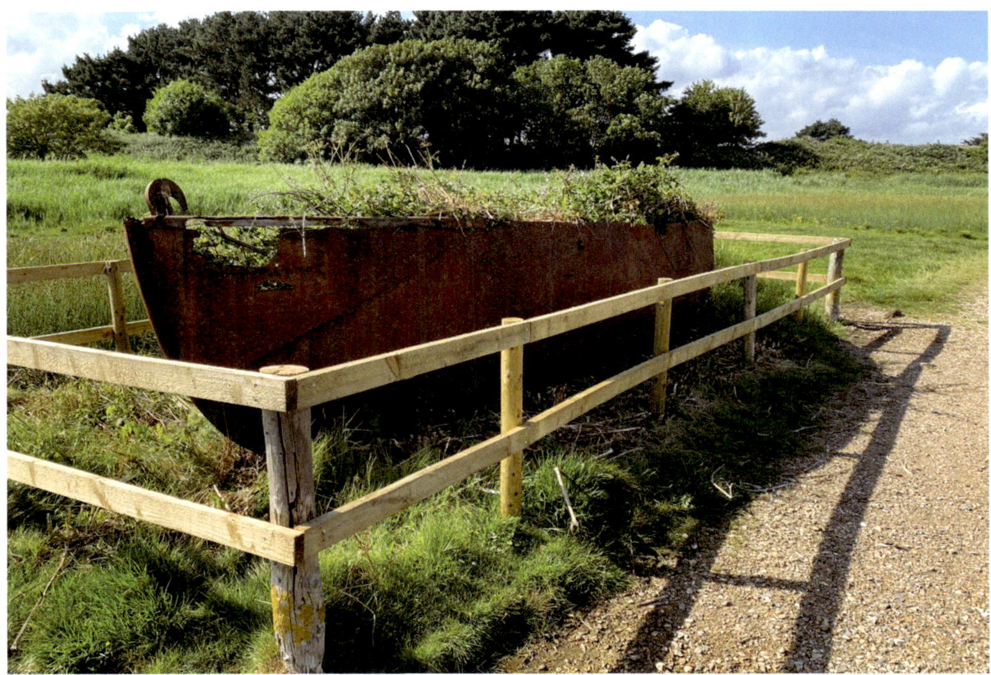

Old iron lifeboat.

Christchurch also became heavily involved in the manufacture of aircraft during the war. It all started in 1940, when a corner of Christchurch Airfield was utilised as an Airspeed factory to produce aircraft for the RAF. This formed part of the government's Shadow Factory scheme, whereby aircraft construction was dispersed throughout the country as a means of increasing manufacturing capability, as well as making the factories harder targets for the Luftwaffe to bomb.

Airspeed was a Portsmouth-based company instigated by aircraft designers AH Titman and NS Norway, the latter being a former protégé of Barnes Wallis of Bouncing Bomb/ Dam Busters fame. Another director was Alan Cobham, a pioneering figure in the world of aviation and later to be the founder of local company Cobham Air Services, which was known for most of its life as Flight Refuelling.

Did You Know?
One of the original founders of Airspeed, AH Titman, went on to achieve fame as an author under the nom de plume of Neville Shute. Prior to this he had made a worthwhile contribution to aviation, having been made a Fellow of the Aeronautical Society for developing a hydraulic retractable undercarriage for the Airspeed Courier.

Initially the Christchurch factory focused on producing the twin-engine Airspeed AS10 Oxford. This aircraft was developed in the late 1930s as the world situation began to look increasingly perilous, prompting the government of the day to request the production of an aircraft capable of training bomber crews. Its maiden flight in 1937 proved successful and it was quickly put into production as the RAF rapidly expanded in preparation for the forthcoming conflict. A total of 8,751 Oxfords were produced, of which 550 were manufactured in Christchurch.

The 'Oxbox' as it was nicknamed was instrumental in training numerous RAF Bomber Command aircrews throughout the Second World War and had the advantage that every element of the crew – i.e. pilots, navigators, bomb aimers, gunners and radio operators – could be trained on the same flight.

Although training was the main forte of the Oxford, they were also used in communications and anti-submarine roles. After the war, Oxfords continued to be useful to the RAF as trainers and light transports and were not withdrawn from service until 1956.

Later in 1940, the pioneer aviator and designer Sir Geoffrey De Havilland acquired Airspeed in order to utilise the factories and skilled workforces. However, the Airspeed name was still retained and the factories operated as subsidiaries of De Havilland.

In 1941, the De Havilland Mosquito came into service. It was constructed predominantly from wood and plywood and was powered by two powerful Rolls-Royce Merlin engines, making it one of the fastest operational aircraft in the world at the time, with a maximum speed in excess of 400 mph.

It was designed as an unarmed bomber with the capability to use speed to escape enemy fighters, but entered service initially as a night fighter.

Nicknamed the 'Wooden Wonder', it became the Allies' premiere night fighter, downing more than 600 Luftwaffe planes as well as intercepting many V1 missiles (the loathed and feared buzz bombs). However, the Mosquito also certainly proved its worth as a bomber with a range of 1,500 miles and a capability of carrying a 4,000-lb bomb load, more than twice the load for which it had been originally designed.

In May 1942, No. 105 Squadron utilised the Mosquito as a daytime bomber. However, their role soon metamorphosed into that of a pathfinder role (by which they marked the targets with flares) within Bomber Command as the RAF ramped up its night bombing offensive. They also sometimes had a role whereby they dropped 4,000-lb blockbuster bombs known as cookies.

The Mosquito's remarkable versatility also allowed it to be used as a high-altitude fighter, or in photo reconnaissance or anti-shipping strikes. They were also often used in specialist roles, for example Operation Jerricho (an attack on Amiens Prison) in 1944 or against other targets such as the Gestapo headquarters.

In 1941, Christchurch Airfield was enlarged and more runways were built, as the airfield adjacent to the factory became RAF Christchurch. It initially operated as an Air Defence Research and Development Establishment, working in conjunction with the Telecommunications Research Establishment at Worth Matravers. The collaboration involved aircraft from RAF Christchurch flying along the Swanage coastline so that their presence could be picked up on a screen as part of a role that was crucial in the two organisations combining to develop radar.

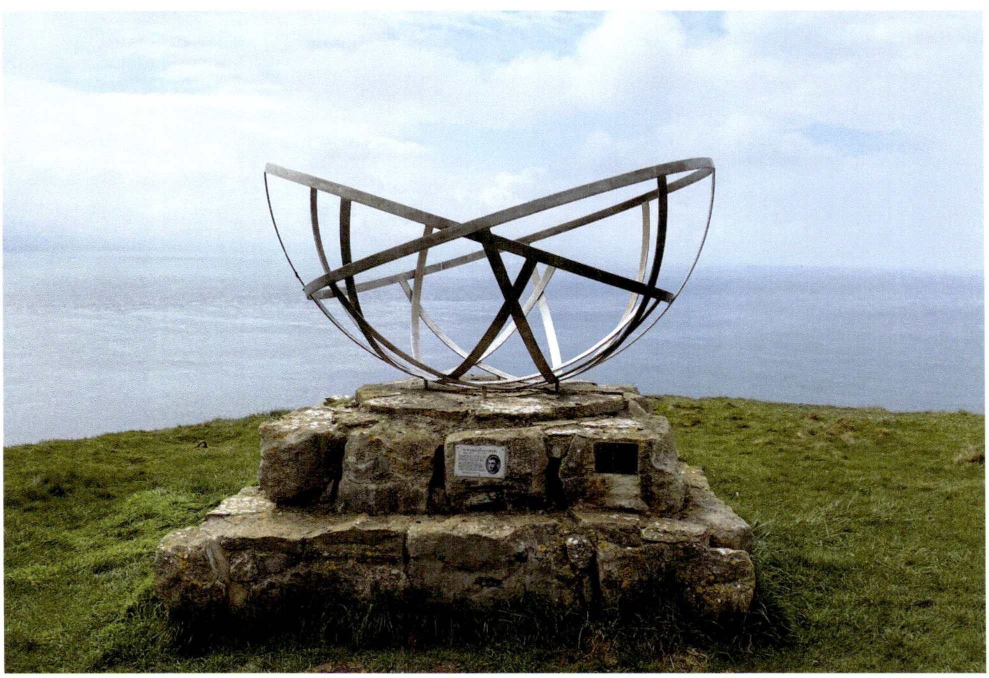

The Worth Matravers Radar Memorial.

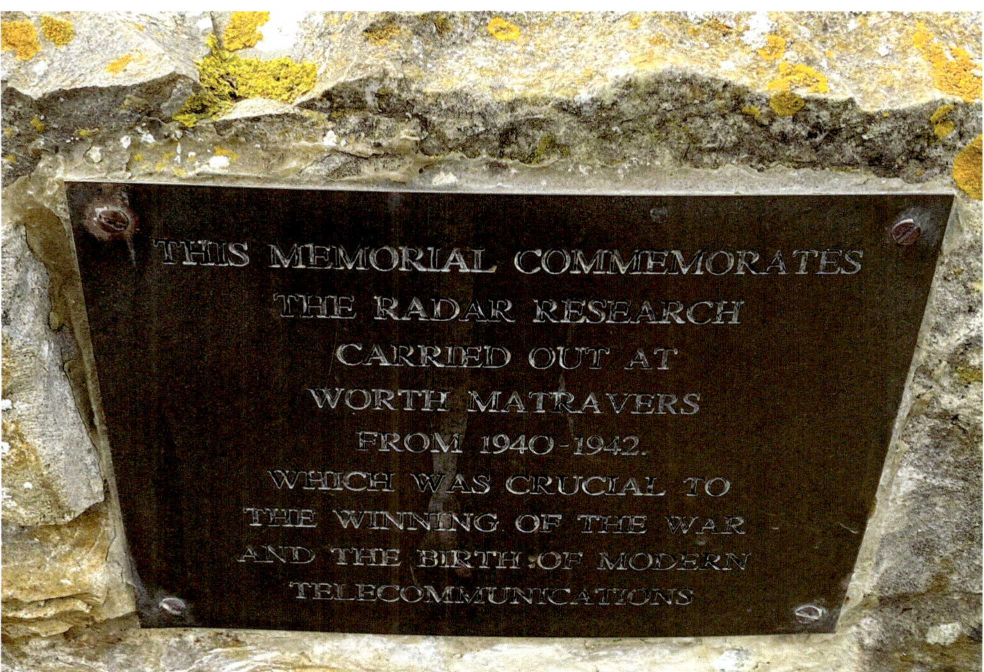

Plaque – The Worth Matravers Radar Memorial.

Also in 1941, a strange incident occurred at RAF Christchurch in the form of a Luftwaffe plane landing on the airfield. The pilots were two intrepid French airmen, Denis Boudard and Jean Herbert, who had been members of the French Air Force serving in Algeria before the force was disbanded in June 1940 after France's surrender to Germany.

Both men returned despondently to their native Caen but vowed to escape German-occupied France and continue the fight from England by joining the Free French Air Force (FFAF). Their ingenious but unconventional plan involved stealing a German plane from Caen Airfield.

They observed the airfield for weeks and identified a two-seater Bucker BU 131, replete with Luftwaffe and swastika markings, that they felt was ripe for their operation. It was a training aircraft with dual controls, which they thought was ideal as they were both novice pilots.

They had noticed that the ground crew at the airfield walked around in black overalls, so they bought something vaguely similar from the local market and dyed them black. Then on the appointed day they strolled up to the aircraft, hamming it up as maintenance men, before eventually working out how to start the thing and getting underway when the opportunity presented itself.

They flew low and headed in the direction of the English Channel, managing to escape radar detection due to their low altitude. However, a warning siren sounded as they flew over Bournemouth which put the RAF on red alert. Undeterred, they spotted Christchurch Airfield and executed a smooth landing, only to be confronted by British airmen brandishing rifles. However, luckily for the valiant Frenchmen, their explanation delivered in broken English was accepted and they were taken to London to join the Free French Air Force.

The ending to the tale is bitter sweet though, as after a campaign in the Middle East with the Free French Air Force, both returned to England. Boudard became an RAF Flight Sergeant and then was the first French airman to land at the re-captured Caen Airfield, before returning to Caen and living to the ripe old age of eighty-five. However, Herbert's return to England resulted in him being tragically shot down and killed by two spitfires who mistook his Miles Master Aircraft for a German Stuka.

As the war progressed, the Spitfire proved to be a very successful aircraft and was very much feared by the Luftwaffe. As a result, it was felt that a naval version that could operate from aircraft carriers would be a useful adjunct and to this end the Seafire was developed, complete with Rolls-Royce Merlin 32 engines. Unfortunately it didn't prove as successful as its airfield-based counterpart, mainly due to the fact that it's undercarriage wasn't that suitable for the task of landing on aircraft carriers. However the Seafire was in operational service from its inception in 1942 until the end of the war and 160 of them were made at Airspeed, Christchurch.

Before the war, Alan Cobham had been approached by Lord Beaverbrook, Minister of Aircraft Production, for assistance in finding new airfields and had no hesitation in recommending Hurn, which comes under Christchurch but is actually equidistant between the towns of Bournemouth and Christchurch. The site was originally intended as a Fighter Command satellite station to RAF Ibsley, but by the time the runways were fully in operation in 1941, there was less demand for fighter airfields, as by then the Battle of Britain had already been won.

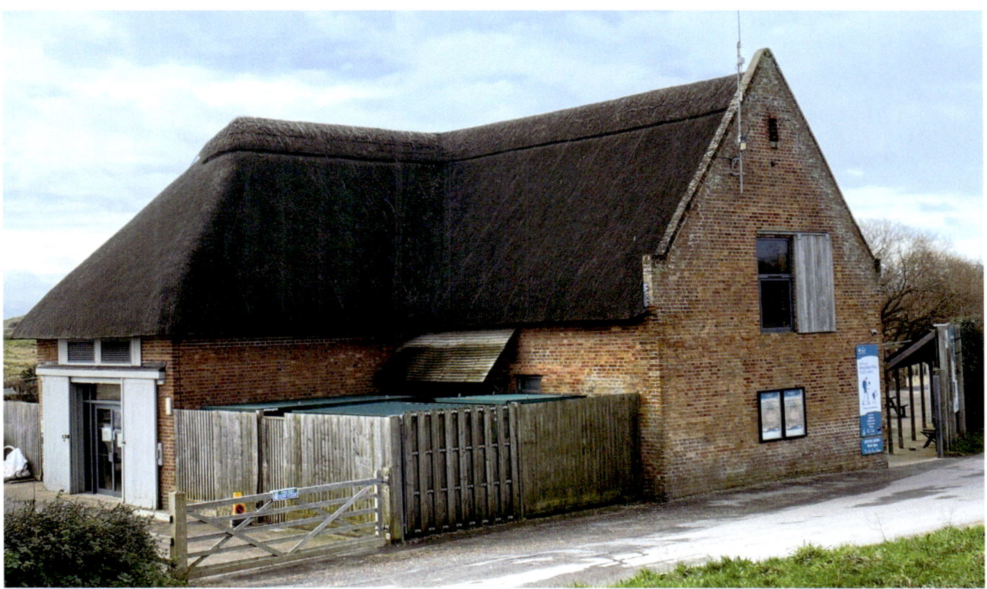

Also in 1941, RAF Southbourne at Hengistbury Head began operating as a Chain Home Radar Station tasked with detecting and identifying enemy bombers. However, apart from a few piles of rubble, all that remains of RAF Southbourne is the former NAAFI which was converted from a Barn Cottage to Hengistbury Head Visitor Centre in 2012.

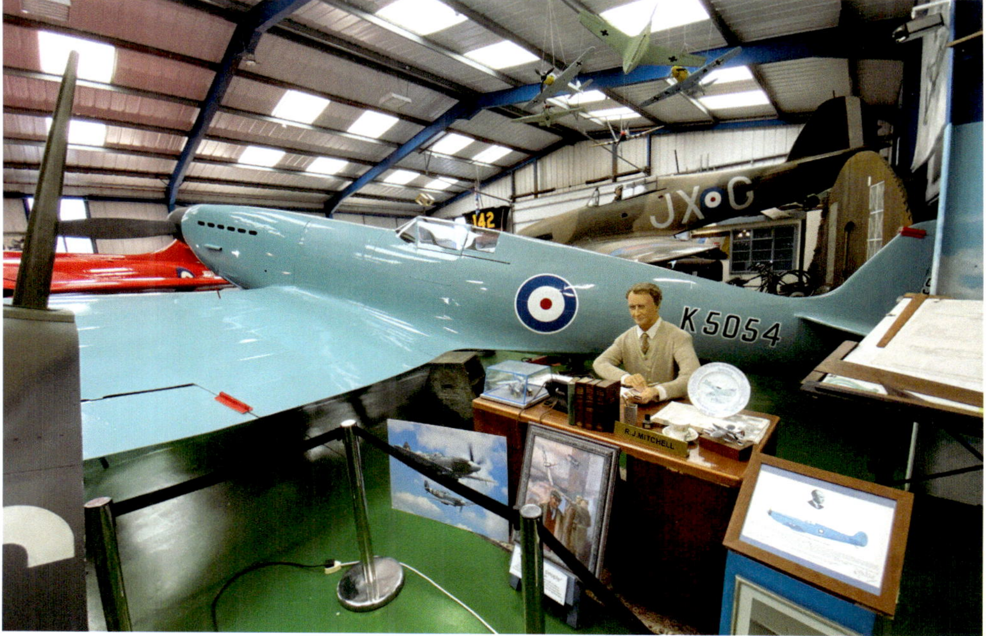

Vickers Supermarine Spitfire (Prototype) Type 300, K5054 Replica. (Published with the permission of Tangmere Military Aviation Museum)

Initially, the airfield was used purely for training purposes. However, the runways were then extended and utilised for transport aircraft, resulting in the airfield becoming very active, as both transport and fighter aircraft including Spitfires, Wellingtons and Typhoons were housed. Subsequently the base took over the radar development role from RAF Christchurch and went on to become instrumental in the development of the use of radar in bombers and fighter bombers supporting the D-Day invasion.

During 1943 and 1944, USAAF took temporary control of several south coast airfields in order to make preparations for their forthcoming role of providing tactical air support to American troops on D-Day.

RAF Hurn became USAAF Station AAF-492 and was home to P-61s of the 422 Night Fighter Squadron, whereas RAF Christchurch became USAAF Station AAF-416, flying P-470 Thunderbolts.

The allies were now very much in the ascendancy and sought to reclaim Europe. Consequently, the Air Ministry called for a glider that was capable of carrying and landing thirty fully equipped paratroopers, the idea being that it would be better for paratroopers to land as a unit behind enemy lines rather than being widely scattered, as would be the case with a conventional parachute drop. As a result, the Airspeed factory adjacent to RAF Christchurch started to produce the Airspeed AS 51 Horsa, named after an Anglo-Saxon warrior. It went from the design shop to production in ten months and 695 of the 3,600 Horsas manufactured nationally were made by Airspeed at Christchurch. The site was unique in that the gliders could also be test flown at the same location.

It was specified that the glider should be a wooden construction to preserve critical supplies of metal, so the framework was predominantly built of spruce and plywood and some of the work was contracted out to local carpentry and furniture making firms who had the required skills.

Operationally, the Horsa was towed by various aircraft including Stirling, Halifax, Albermarle and later the Dakota. It saw action in Sicily in 1943, and then crucially in the D-Day landings, where they were instrumental in the Allies securing the strategically important bridge at Benouville, over the Caen Canal in Normandy (also known as Pegasus Bridge).

Following the Normandy assault, the Horsa was used in Operation Dragon (Invasion of Provence, southern France) on 15 August 1944, Operation Market Garden (Arnhem) in September 1944 and Operation Varsity (Allied crossing of the Rhine) on 24 March 1945.

Possibly, Hurn's most famous D-Day flyer was known as Paddy the Pigeon. He was one of thousands of messenger pigeons donated by pigeon fanciers to help the war effort. Thirty pigeons, including Paddy, were specially selected for D-Day missions. They were delivered to RAF Hurn prior to being taken to France by a unit of the First US Army.

After his release at 8.15 a.m. on 12 June 1944, Paddy returned to Hurn in a record-breaking time of 4 hours and 50 minutes with vital coded information on the Allied advance. This was the fastest time ever recorded by a message-carrying pigeon, and in appreciation of his outstanding contribution, Paddy was awarded the Dicken Medal, the animal equivalent of the Victoria Cross.

After the war Paddy was reunited with his owner in his home town of Carnlough, Northern Ireland, where he enjoyed a more peaceful time until he died in 1954, aged eleven. Paddy achieved recognition as a hero, but many of his brave pigeon comrades were killed in the line of duty as they flew through the dangerous skies to deliver their messages.

After D-Day, Christchurch was handed back to the RAF and Hurn also reverted to its RAF Transport role.

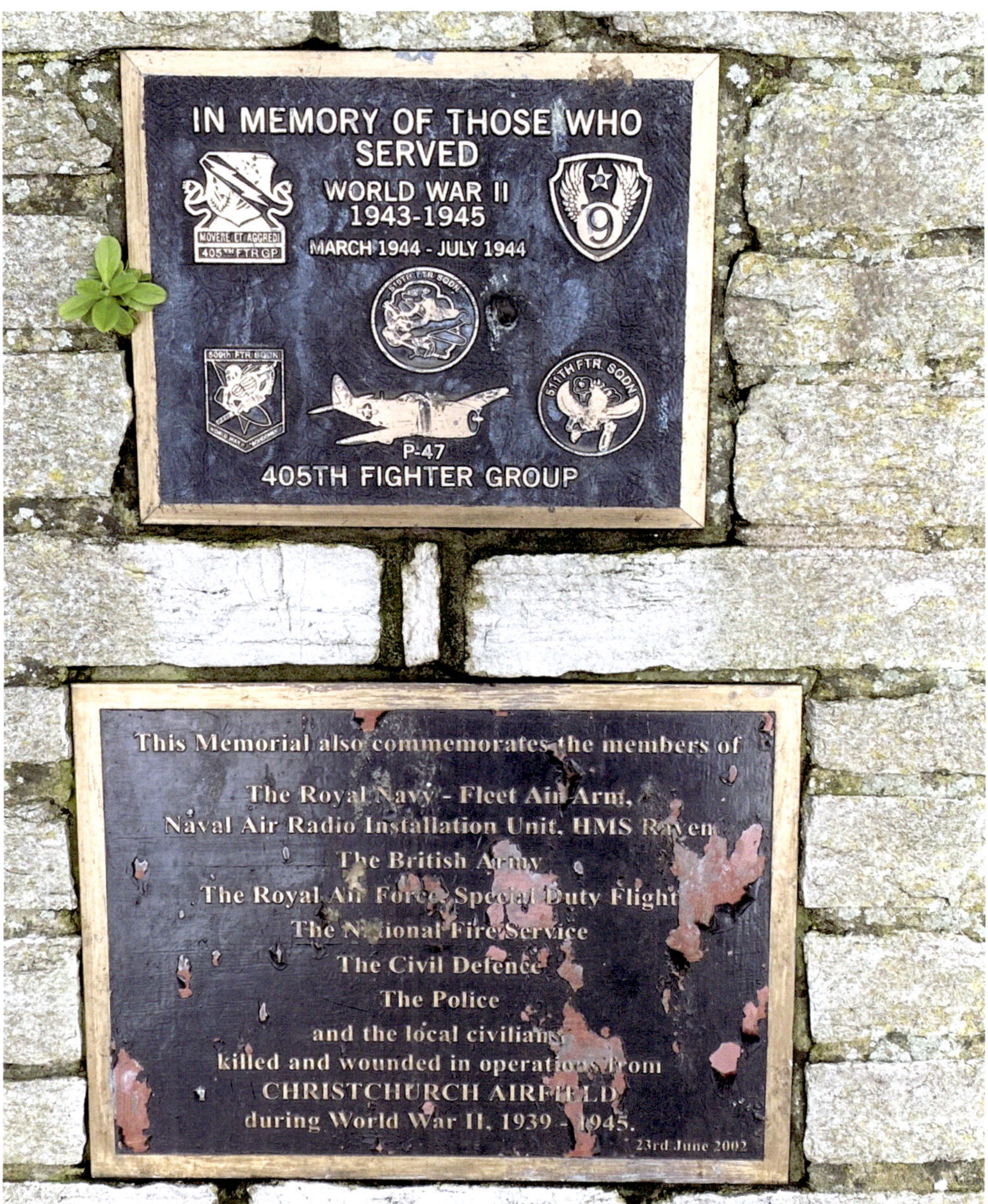

Remembrance plaques – Second World War.

5. Post-war Aviation and Aircraft Manufacture

By the end of the war, De Havilland had evolved to become a major name in the world of aircraft manufacture and was now utilising the airfield at Christchurch, adjacent to the factory, for test flying of the military jet fighters and civilian airliners which they were now producing. However, although De Havilland now owned majority shares, the aircraft built at both Portsmouth and Christchurch still continued to be manufactured under the banner of Airspeed.

Airspeed at Christchurch had very successfully manufactured Mosquitoes during the war and this continued post-war until 1950. However, De Havilland/Airspeed then moved into the commercial airline market, producing Airspeed A557 Ambassadors which were initially powered by two Bristol Hercules engines, before they were upgraded with more powerful Bristol Centaurus engines.

British European Airways (BEA) placed an order for twenty in 1952 as they were keen to utilise the Ambassador's pressurised cabins and excellent soundproofing in order to develop an upmarket Elizabethan Class of airline travel, named in honour of the newly crowned queen. The concept proved very successful and additional routes were soon established, making the Airspeed AS57 Ambassador, often now known as the Elizabethan, BEA's most used aircraft.

However the initial popularity of the aircraft waned as turbo prop aircraft, like the Vickers Viscount, made down the road at Hurn, were introduced. Consequently, Ambassadors were gradually withdrawn from service and production ceased in 1953. The final nail in the coffin came as a result of the negative publicity generated in the aftermath of the Munich Air Disaster on 6 February 1958 involving Manchester United's Busby Babes.

In 1948, De Havilland took over the Airspeed factory completely, consigning the Airspeed name to the history books. The focus then became military aircraft rather than commercial airliners and production continued to the extent that in 1954 the factory was a major company locally with over 2,000 people employed.

Meanwhile, the area had become the home of Britain's first international land-based airport, taking over from neighbouring Poole, which throughout the war and until 1948 had become a sea-based international airport through its utilisation of Flying Boats at Salterns Marina, Lilliput.

British Airways Overseas Corporation (BOAC) employed 600 staff at Poole to support their various flight crews and flying boat services. In addition to Salterns, other premises were requisitioned at Poole Pottery and on the Quay to provide back-up services, such as administration and cargo storage. RAAF 461 and RAF 210 squadrons from RAF Transport Command were also based at Poole.

The civilian flying boats were moored on the water and passengers, mail and freight were ferried to them from launches, before takeoff from the water. There were twelve high-speed launches, with sixty staff operating them.

At this time, Salterns was Britain's only international airport and famous passengers have included royalty, test cricketers, various film stars and politicians including Winston Churchill.

After the war, Salterns returned to its former use as a marina and Poole Harbour Yacht Club took over. Today Poole is recognised as the birthplace of BOAC and the forerunner of British Airways.

However, by 1944 USAAF had handed back control of Hurn to the RAF and the base returned to an air transport role. Shortly afterwards, in May 1945, control transferred to the Ministry of Civil Aviation, who were keen to utilise the airfield's longer runways. This was the birth of Bournemouth International Airport, which was Britain's first international land-based airport, although, initially, as had been the case at Poole during the war, the flights were for government officials or military VIPs and not the general public. At this time, BOAC were operating regular flights to Sydney using converted Lancaster bombers, then shortly afterwards transatlantic services from New York were operated by Pan Am using DC4 Skymasters and Constellations.

Bournemouth remained Britain's main international airport until the canvas structure that was London Heathrow took over the premier role when it was upgraded in March 1946, with all BOAC flights relocated there. However, Bournemouth continued to play a role, during the 1940s and 1950s, as a site that could accommodate flights that had been diverted from Heathrow and therefore continued to receive flights from around the world.

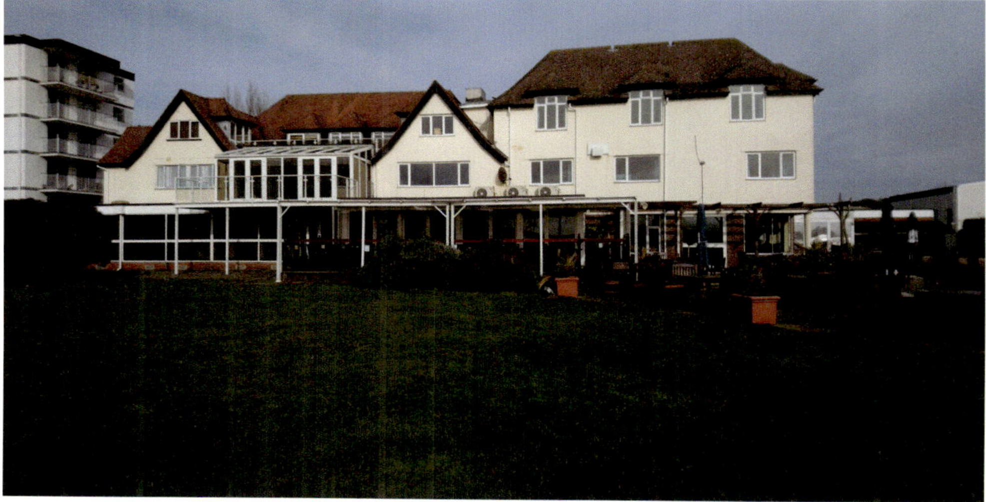

Salterns Hotel at Salterns Marina, Lilliput, Poole, was formerly the BOAC Marine Terminal – Salterns and Britain's first international airport.

In the 1950s local services were introduced from Bournemouth to the Channel Islands, Paris, Manchester and Glasgow. During this time also, Silver City Services began operating airline car ferry services, but these were curtailed in 1966 with the advent of 'roll on roll off' car ferries.

Also during this period, Bournemouth International Airport became a major centre of aircraft manufacture when Vickers Armstrong moved into the site, precipitating a thirty-year stint, during which 146 Varsities, 279 Viscounts and 222 BAC 1-11s rolled off the production line.

The first of these was the Vickers Varsity, which was a twin-engine crew trainer operated by the RAF from 1951 to 1976. It was developed from the Vickers Valetta and was built to replace the Vickers Wellington T10 as a heavy aircraft crew trainer.

The Varsity served the RAF well before being withdraw from service in May 1976, when it was replaced as a pilot trainer by the Scottish Aviation Jetstream T1 and as a navigation trainer by the Hawker Siddeley Dominie T1.

The Viscount then entered service in 1953, as a revolutionary passenger aircraft which featured two Rolls-Royce turbo prop Dart engines, making it faster, smoother and quieter than its contemporaries. Accordingly, it was very popular with passengers, who also appreciated the large windows. Many orders were received from all over the world, resulting in the Bournemouth site being chosen as an additional production centre.

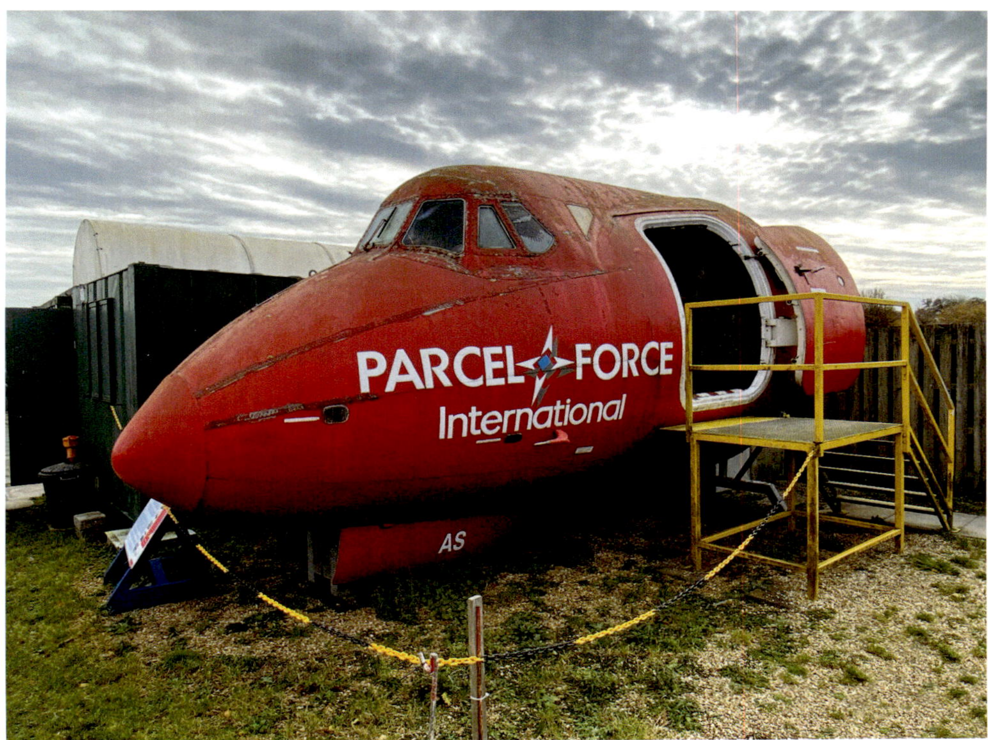

The nose section of a Viscount. (Published with the permission of Bournemouth Aviation Museum)

Viscounts also flew from Bournemouth International Airport and were operated by many different airlines including BEA, Cambrian, Dan Air and British United. Production continued until 1964, but the aircraft were still operational until the 1980s with some being converted to cargo planes and the last remaining flying Viscounts finally being retired in South Africa in 2007.

In the meantime, Christchurch Aero Club reopened, as did a glider school on the south-western area of the airfield. Later in 1953, De Havilland located its Apprentice School at Christchurch, occupying what had been Somerford Theatre in Somerford Way. Among the group of actors that had performed at the theatre was a group who formed the New Forest Coven of Witches. The building was built in 1938, but was destroyed by a fire in 1975.

In the period from the 1950s to the mid-1960s, De Havilland, Christchurch, manufactured three distinctive twin-boom military fighters: the Vampire, the Venom and the Sea Vixen.

The first was the Vampire, which followed on from the Second World War Mosquito and had a front wooden fuselage with a De Havilland Goblin engine mounted behind the pilot. It proved to be a highly successful aircraft and over 3,000 of all versions were built.

The Vampire Trainer T11 was built at Christchurch from 1950, for use by the RAF and other overseas air forces. The RAF utilised the plane in Training Command, but it was also used as a continuation trainer in other units including Fighter Command squadrons. The plane was the second jet fighter to enter service with the RAF after the Meteor. Bournemouth Airport also played a role by undertaking final testing and test flights.

The Vampire also operated in a role as a fighter bomber until 1953, although it still remained as a training aircraft. Furthermore more specialist ground attack and fighter versions continued in RAF service until 1966, when they were finally withdrawn from RAF training programmes and replaced by the Folland Gnat, as used by the Red Arrows before the introduction of the Hawk.

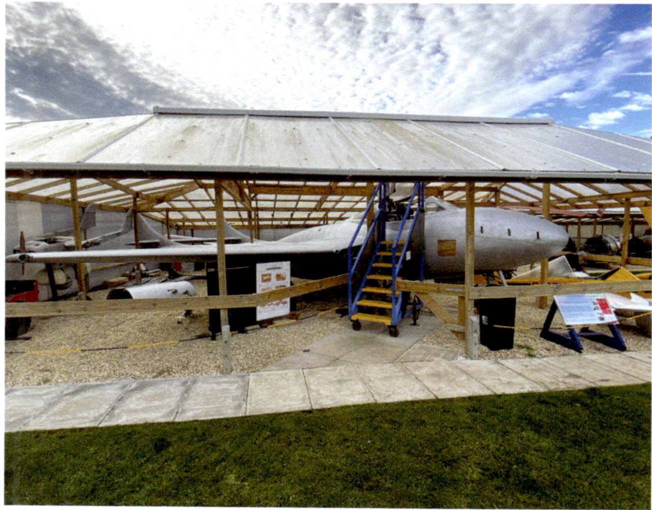

This Vampire T11 is in the process of being lovingly restored at Bournemouth Aviation Museum. Progress was initially severely hampered by the elements – hence the need for the specially built protective shelter. This version is a 1950s trainer and has a De Havilland Goblin engine. This one was actually built at Hatfield not Christchurch. However, the De Havilland factory at Christchurch did build T11s. (Published with the permission of Bournemouth Aviation Museum)

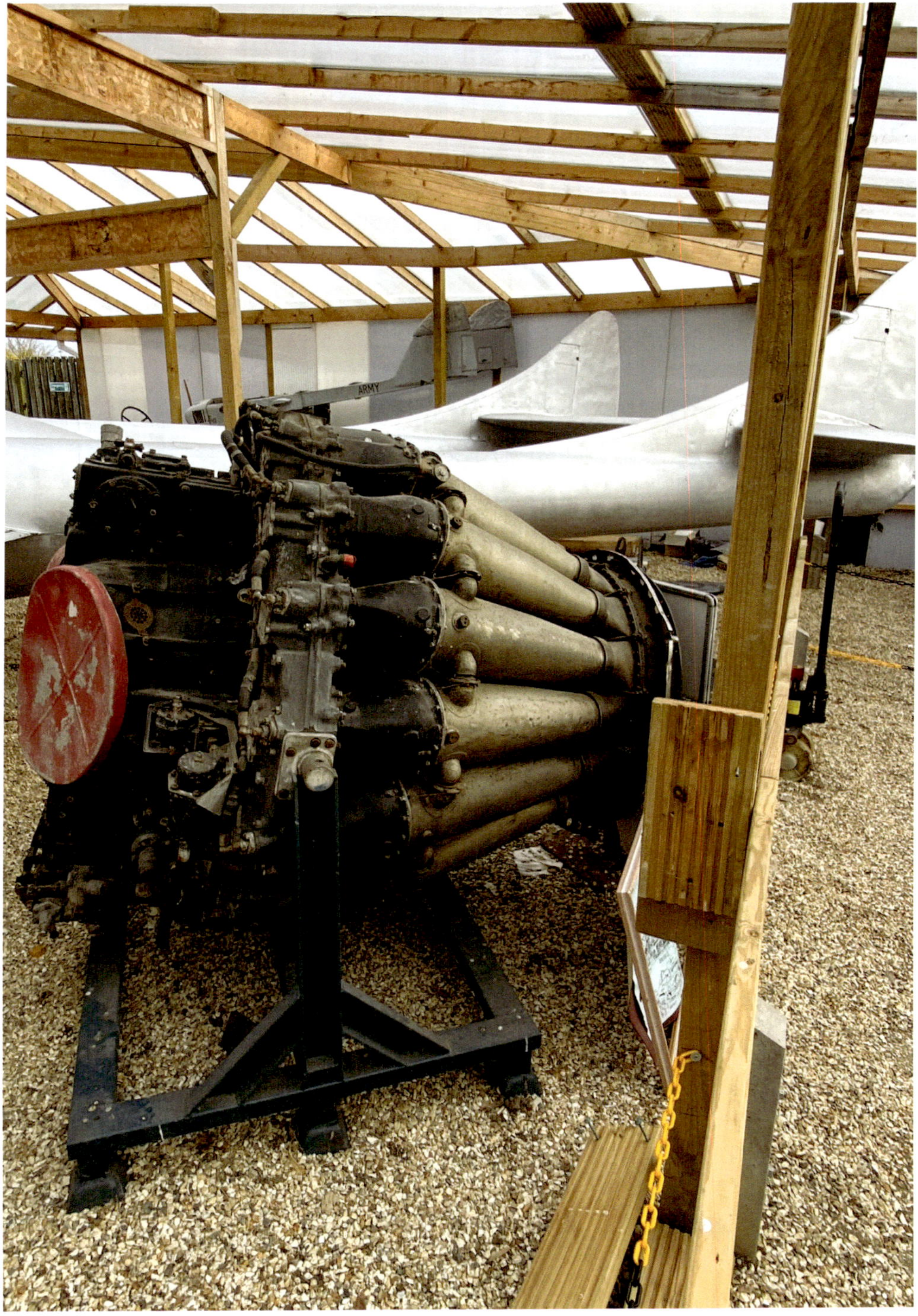

The De Havilland Goblin engine, as used in the Vampire. This one is the actual engine from the Vampire on display. (Published with the permission of Bournemouth Aviation Museum)

In 1953, the replacement for the Vampire was the Venom, which was utilised by the RAF as a night fighter. Although similar in appearance to the Vampire, it had a more powerful De Havilland Ghost engine, giving it 50 per cent more thrust, making it faster. It also had twice the range as well as the capability of carrying a greater weapons payload.

The later variant, the Sea Venom, was a version adapted for aircraft carrier use and included such features as a folding wing, strengthened undercarriage and a tail hook.

The Sea Venom served with the Royal Navy until 1959, when it was gradually replaced by the Sea Vixen, both of which were also widely exported.

Did You Know?
Between 1984 and 2000 a Sea Vixen FAW 2 (XJ 500) was on public display as a visual reminder of Christchurch's great aircraft manufacturing heritage. However, it was removed for safe keeping and has now found its way to Tangmere Museum of Military Aviation, where it has been fully restored and is displayed in its original 899 NAS colours from when it was operational on HMS *Eagle* in 1970.

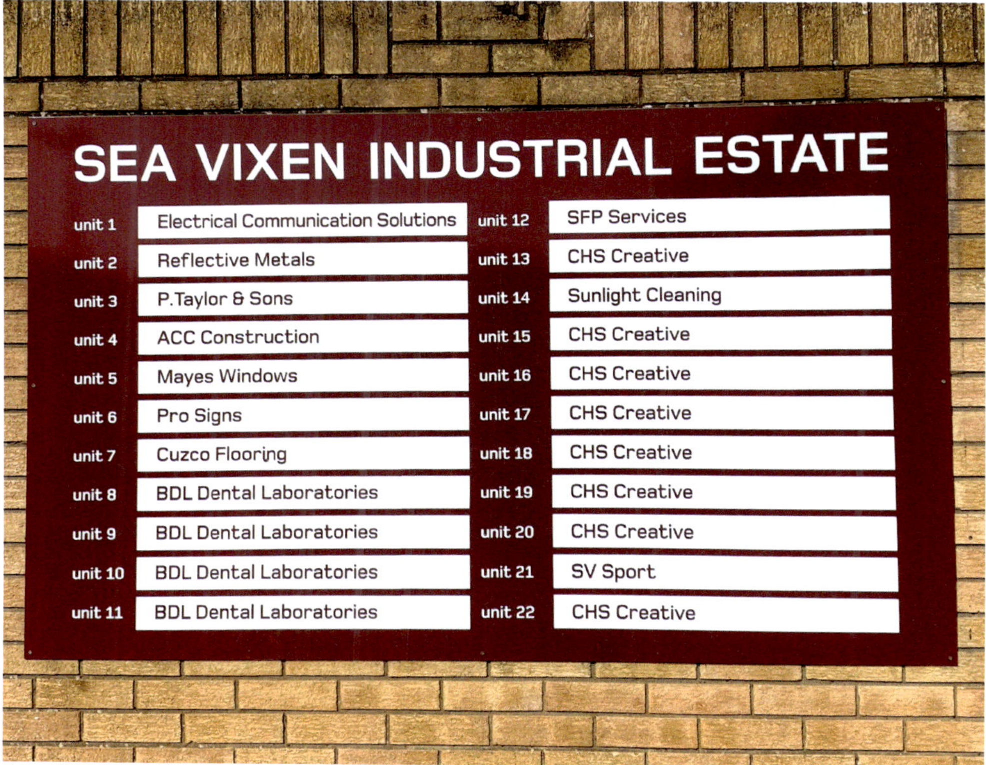

A noticeboard at the Sea Vixen Industrial Estate.

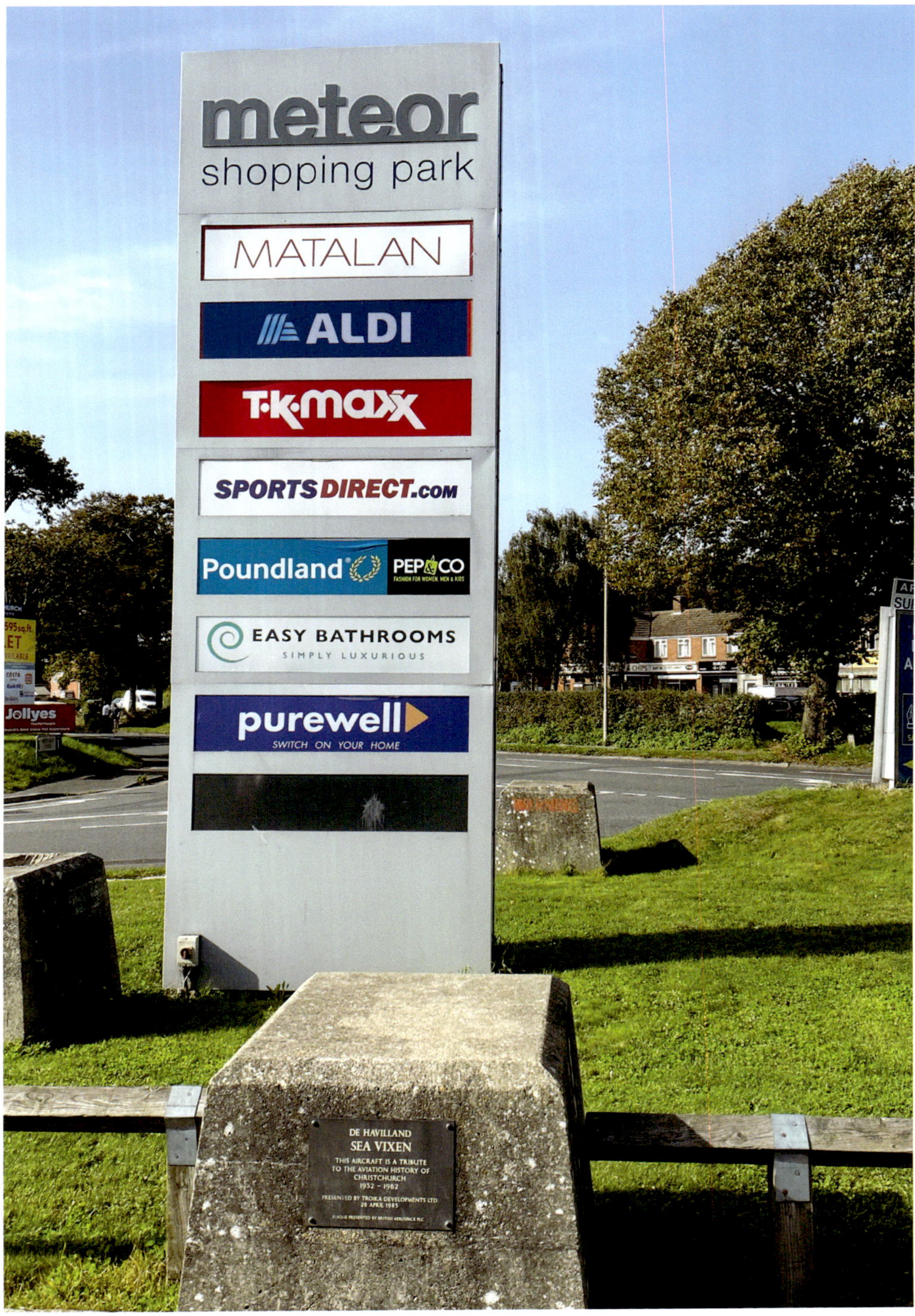

This plaque is situated on one of the concrete plinths on which the Sea Vixen that was on public display in Christchurch used to stand.

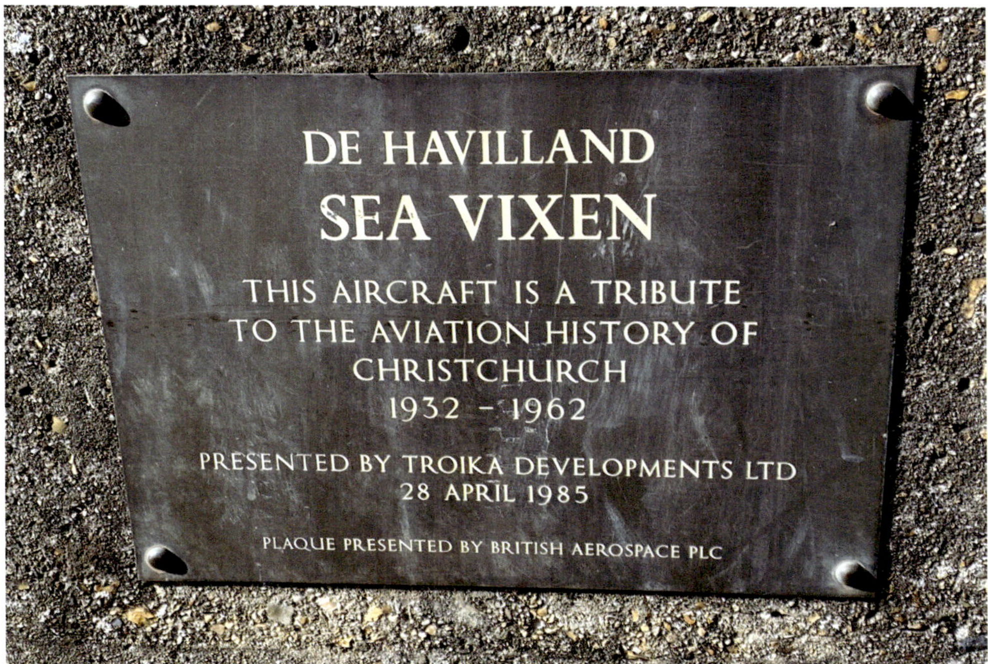

Plaque – Sea Vixen.

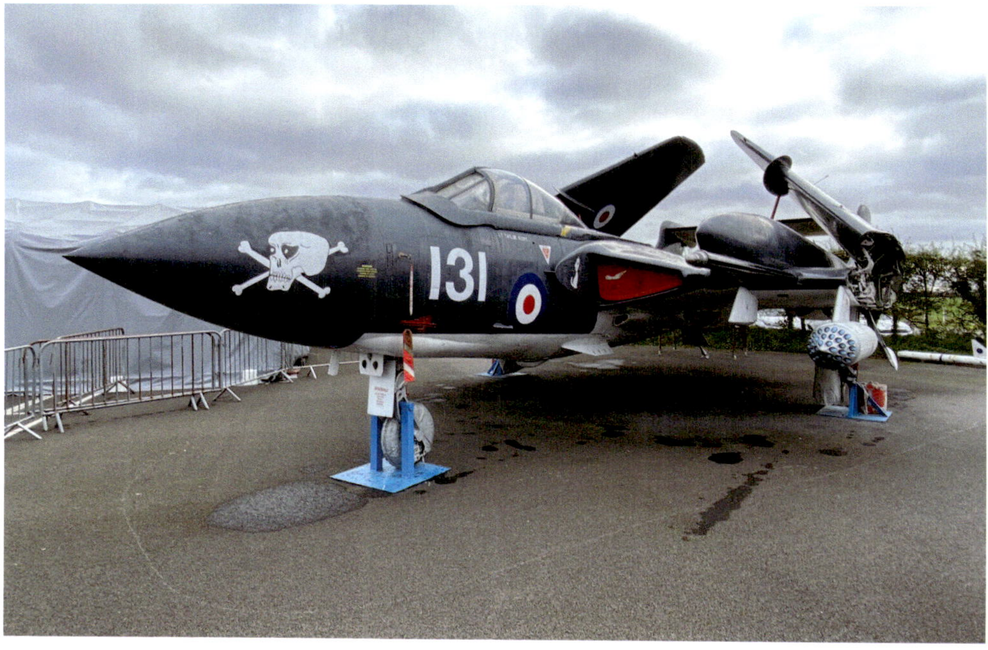

The beast now resides at Tangmere having previously rested on the concrete plinths at Christchurch. (Published with the permission of Tangmere Military Aviation Museum)

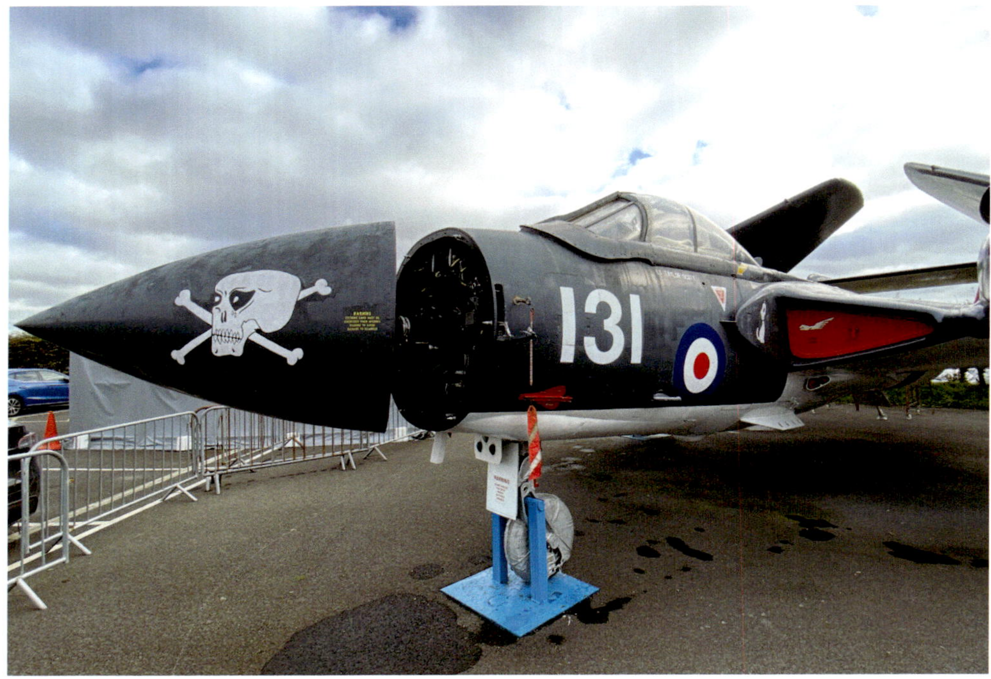

Sea Vixen – nose cone open. (Published with the permission of Tangmere Military Aviation Museum)

The Sea Vixen was a Fleet Air Arm, aircraft carrier-based jet fighter, introduced into service in 1959 and retired in 1972. It was a much larger aircraft than the Venom or the Vampire and was powered by two Rolls-Royce Avon engines. It was capable of supersonic speed and saw combat in Tanganyika and during the Aden emergency.

Did You Know?
The last airworthy De Havilland Vixen currently sits outside the Fleet Air Arm Museum at Yeovilton. However, it is due to be transferred to Bournemouth Aviation Museum for renovation and display, having been seriously damaged at Yeovilton during a wheels-up landing.

The De Havilland site finally closed in 1962, resulting in the adjacent airfield falling into disuse, before subsequently making way for housing and the Runway Industrial site. Today there are very few reminders of its previous incarnation. However, some of the Airspeed/De Havilland original factory units still stand on Somerford Road, although they are now used for other purposes.

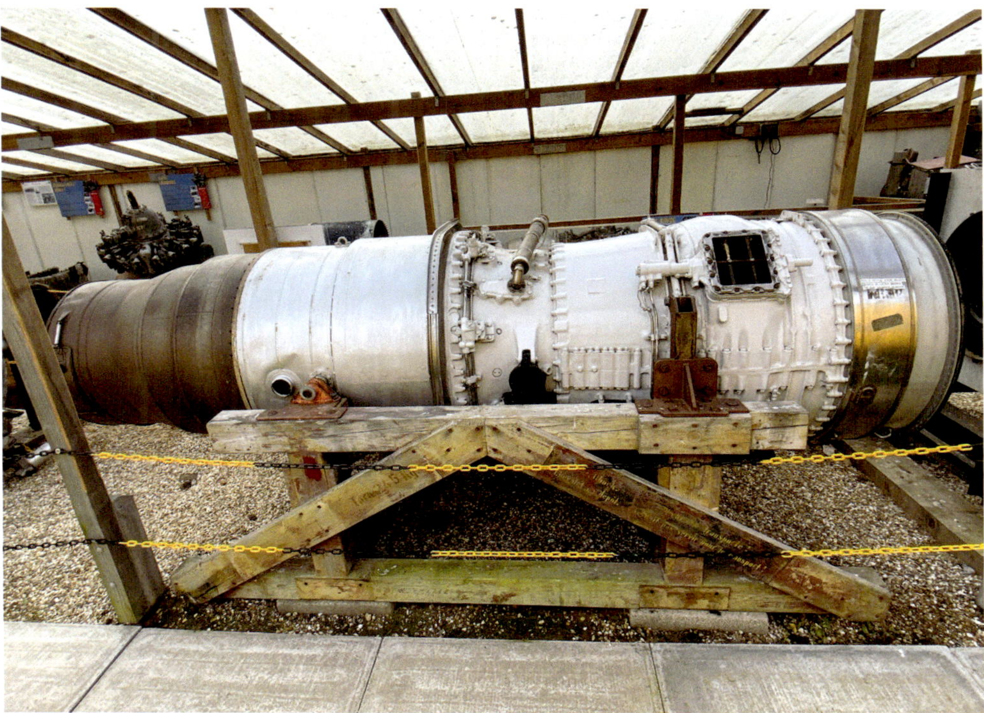

This particular Rolls-Royce Avon engine was used in the Hawker Hunter, but an improved version was later used in the Sea Vixen as well as later models of the Vampire. (Published with the permission of Bournemouth Aviation Museum)

However aircraft production still continued at Bournemouth Airport, where the Viscount was followed up with the BAC 1-11, which was a short-haul aircraft and another fantastic export winner. It was powered by two rear fuselage-mounted Rolls-Royce Spey engines. It had a range of 2,000 miles and a passenger seating capacity of eighty-nine. The first prototype flew from Bournemouth Airport on 20 August 1963 and it was in use by commercial airlines by 1965.

The manufacture of the BAC 1-11 was a joint effort by a number of different sites. Filton built the rear fuselage and tail, Weybridge the centre section and undercarriage, and Luton the wings. Meanwhile, Hurn (BAC always referred to the factory as Hurn rather than Bournemouth Airport) produced the main fuselage and also undertook final assembly, the site having proved its capability during the production of the highly successful Vickers Viscount.

The noisy Rolls-Royce Spey engines proved the aircraft's undoing and resulted in it being finally withdrawn from service after European and North American noise regulations came into effect on 1 April 2002. The final commercial flight took place from Bournemouth Airport the day before, but by then, the Hurn factory had already closed after the sale of the last BAC 1-11 in 1984.

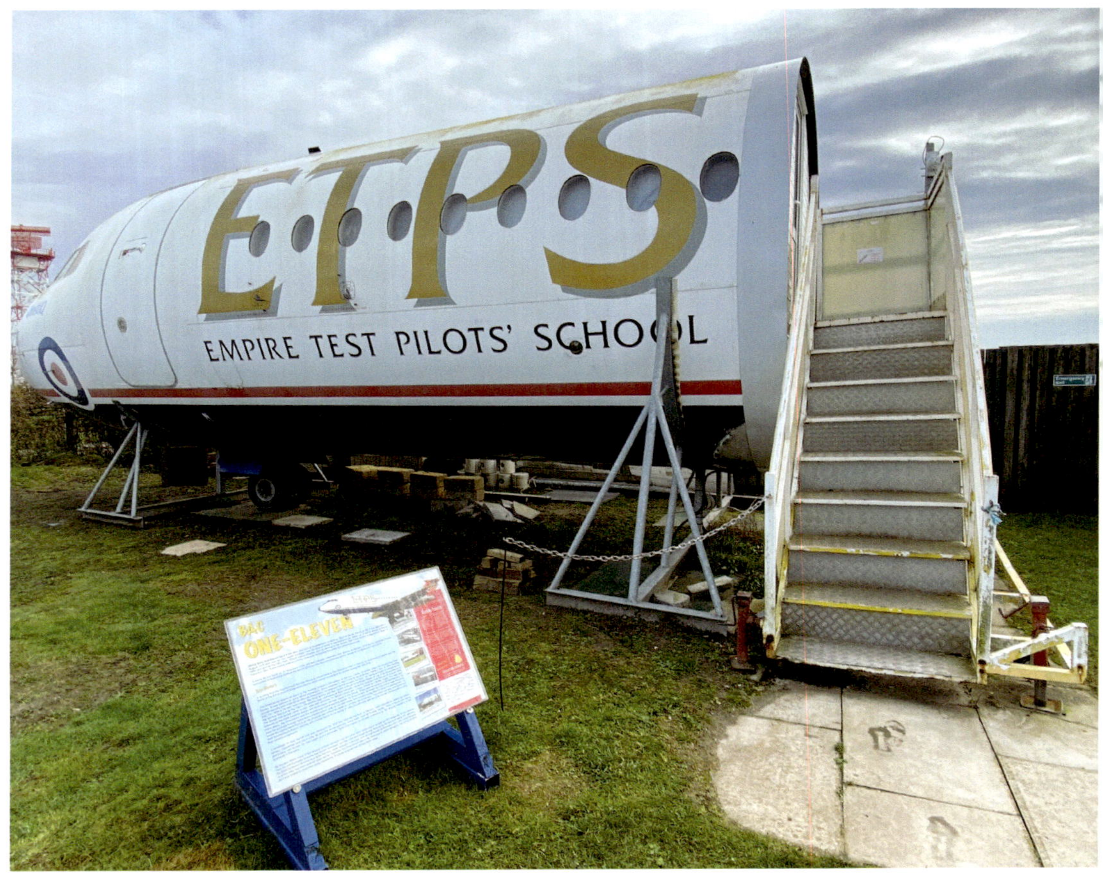

This section of a BAC 1-11 ZE432 is a 400 series built at Bournemouth Airport in 1973 and was one of seventy-four ordered by Air Pacific of Fiji. It was used for inter-island services, operating from airfields with short runways – just the kind of function the design was ideally suited for. The aircraft was also popular with package holiday operators including Bournemouth Airport-based Palmair. In March 1984, this particular model was taken out of service and sold to the UK Ministry of Defence for use at the Empire Test Pilots' School at Boscombe Down, Old Sarum, Salisbury, where it was in use until November 2009. (Published with the permission of Bournemouth Aviation Museum)

The British aviation industry as a whole now largely focuses on components and systems rather than complete aircraft, but still remains one of the world's largest aerospace industries. In the present day, at Bournemouth International Airport, many of the factories and hangars still continue with aviation-related activities and the manufacture of aircraft components. One example is Curtiss Wright, who specialise in avionics and electronics, making items such as black box flight recorders.

Another operator is BAE Systems at the Grange Road Business Park, who were formerly British Aerospace, having previously been Hawker Siddeley from 1960 and before that De Havilland.

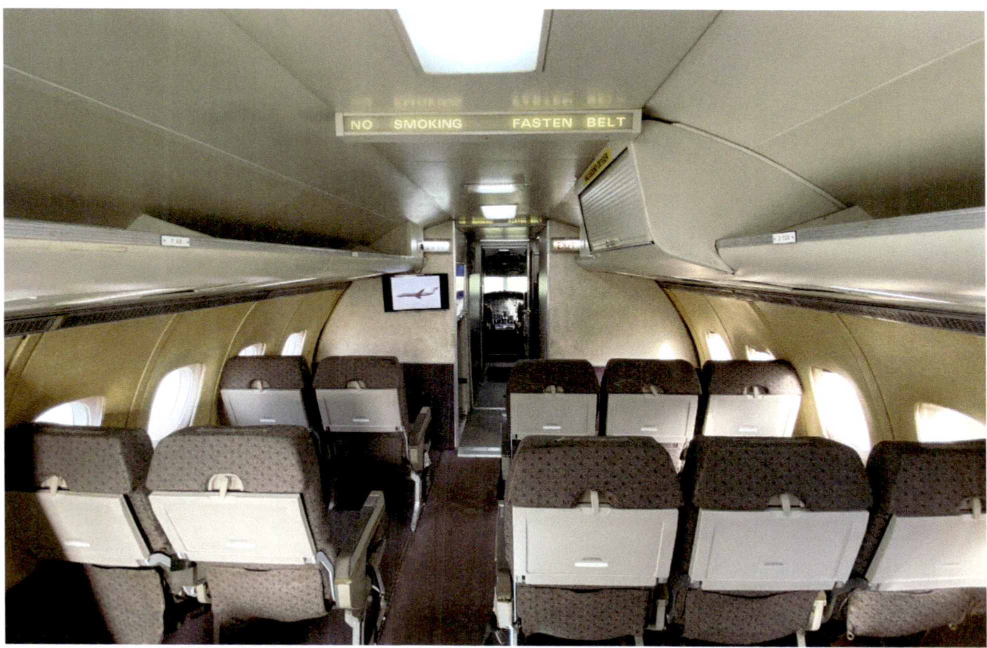

BAC 1-11 passenger seating. This exhibit is often used for meetings, instruction, movies and photo shoots. (Published with the permission of Bournemouth Aviation Museum)

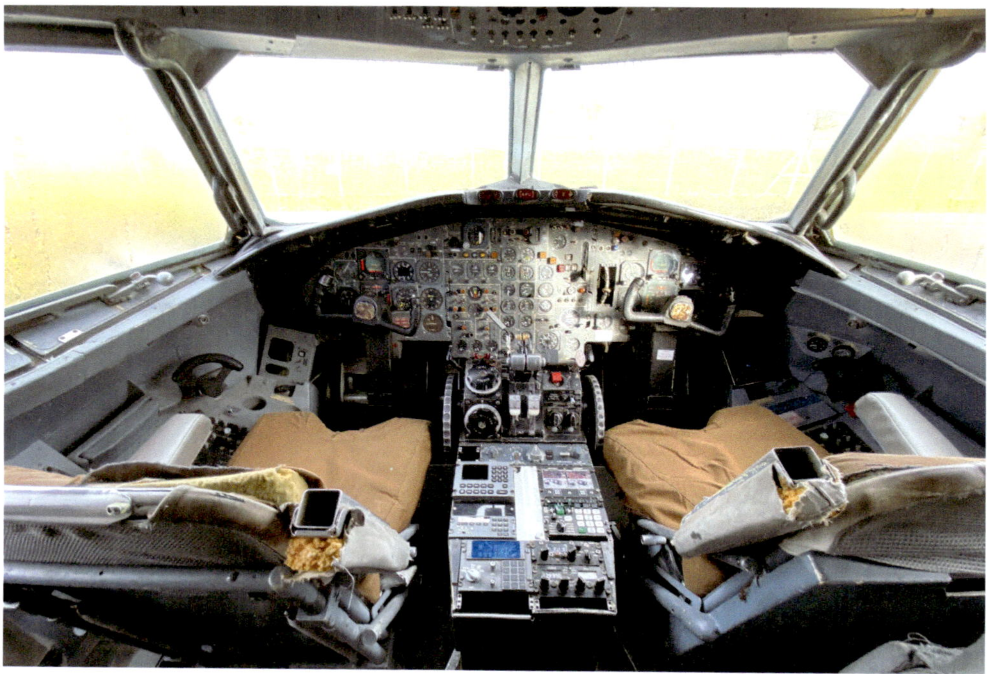

BAC 1-11 cockpit. (Published with the permission of Bournemouth Aviation Museum)

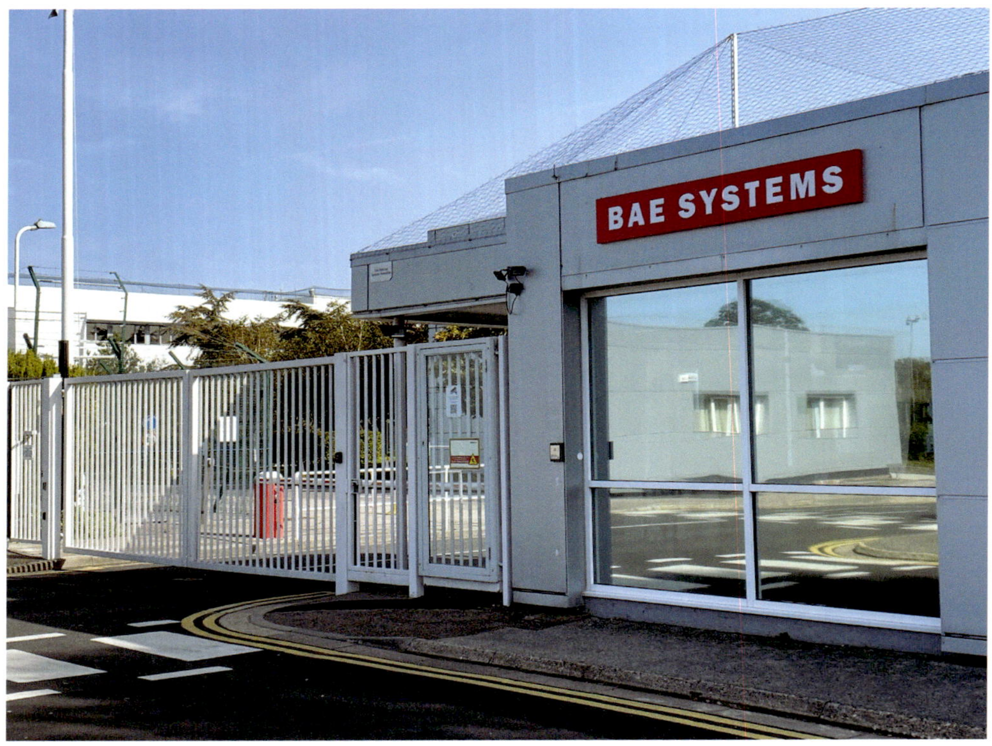

BAE Systems.

A further Christchurch player in the aerospace sector is Beagle Technology Group in Stony Lane, who were founded in 1956 and currently design and manufacture metallic and composite parts and structures as well as components for the aerospace industry.

Yet another local firm established in 1934 and based at Bournemouth Airport as well as at Wimborne is the previously alluded to Cobham Aviation Services (*see* Pre-war Aviation and the Second World War, Including Aviation and Aircraft Manufacture). The company was founded by Alan Cobham in 1943 and was originally called Flight Refuelling, changing its name in November 1994. The original concept and purpose of the organisation, as the original name of the company suggests, was to enable aeroplanes to refuel whilst in flight. Initial trials in the late 1940s involved a Lancaster bomber as a tanker refuelling a Gloster Meteor. The system proved successful and was sold to the RAF and USAAF.

During 1954, Michael Cobham, Alan's son, began to diversify the company and in 1985, Cobham became a public limited company, with the Cobham family still retaining the vast majority of shares.

The company's services were particularly useful in the Falklands conflict of 1982, as their wealth of knowledge, know-how and experience was vital in refuelling aircraft and allowing them to travel the vast distances from Britain to Ascension Island and then onwards to the Falklands in the South Atlantic.

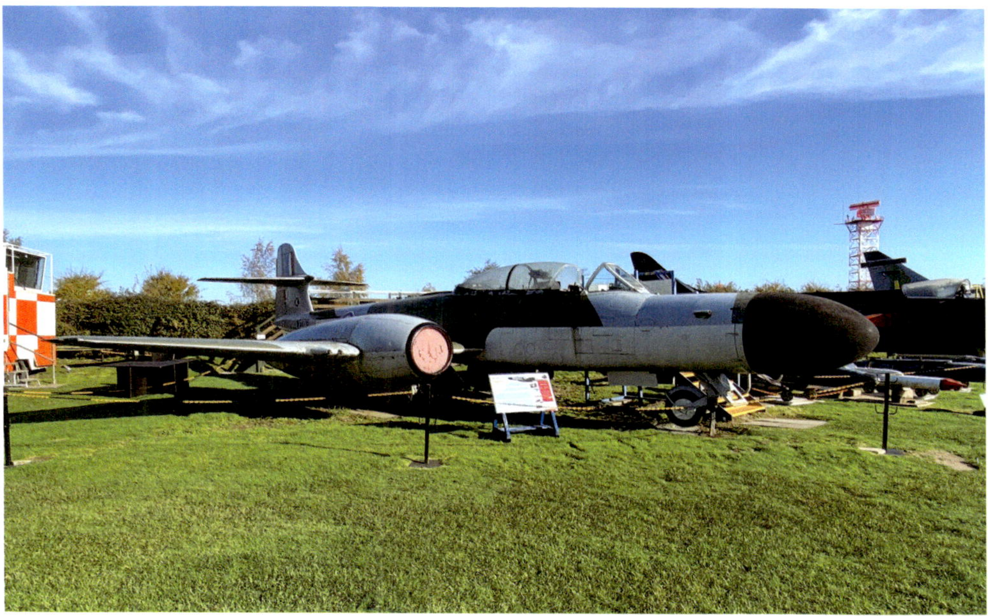

Gloster Meteors were used in early flight refuelling trials in the late 1940s and then were used as target drones in threat simulation roles on naval exercises, as Flight Refuelling Ltd diversified in the 1960s and 1970s. (Published with the permission of Bournemouth Aviation Museum)

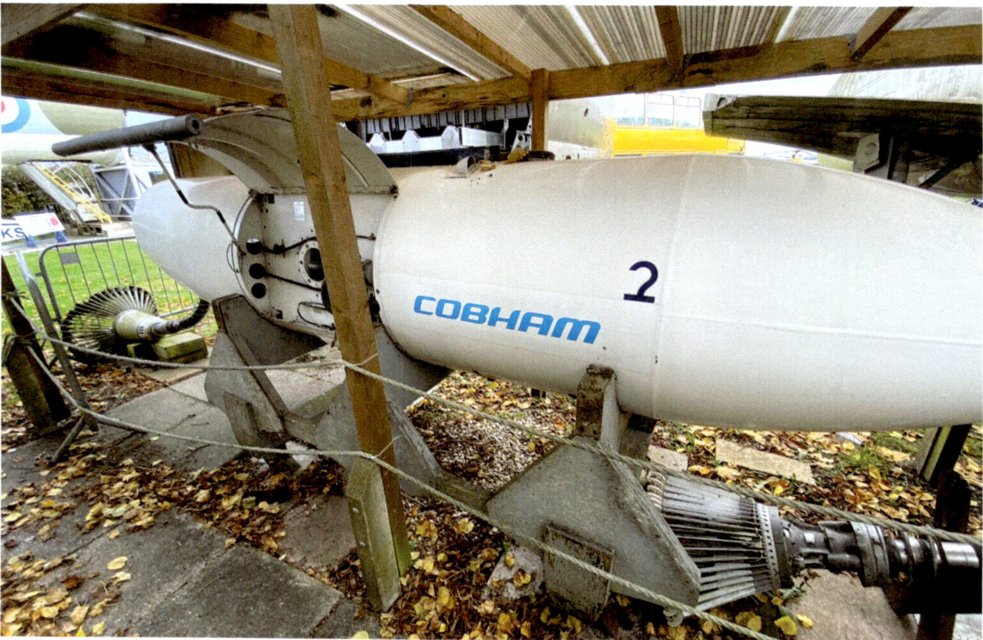

Cobham flight refuelling equipment. (Published with the permission of Bournemouth Aviation Museum)

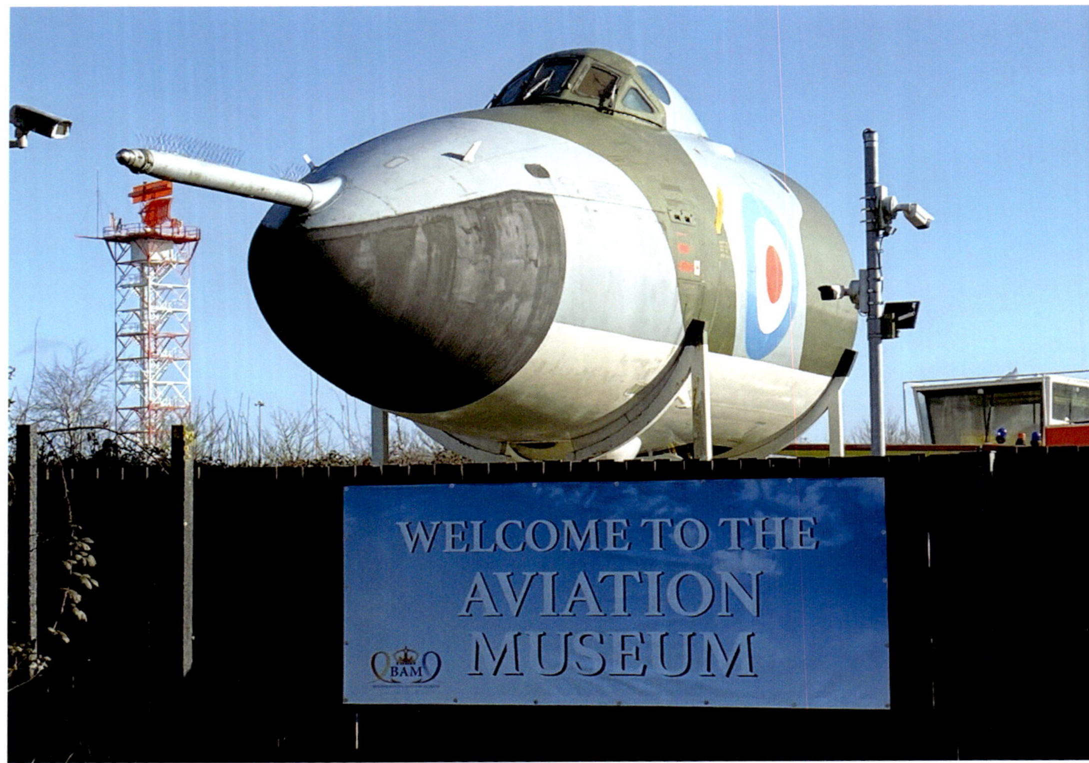

The nose section of a Vulcan. The iconic bomber was hastily brought back into service for the Falklands conflict of 1982, having just been retired. Two Vulcans were sent out from Ascension Island to bomb the runway of Port Stanley Airport 4,000 miles away. This meant flying for fifteen hours with numerous in-flight refuelling enabled by Cobham flight refuelling systems, allowing the Vulcans to deliver their payload of twenty 1,000-lb bombs. The same system also supported Harriers on numerous occasions. (Published with the permission of Bournemouth Aviation Museum)

After the Falklands, the Wimborne factory received a visit from Air Commander, South Atlantic Air Marshall Sir John Curtiss and Prime Minister Margaret Thatcher to offer official recognition, appreciation and thanks for their efforts during the conflict.

In 1994, the firm was renamed Cobham plc in acknowledgment of the company's founder, before later becoming Cobham Aviation Services in recognition of the fact that the firm was now providing operational readiness training, mission rehearsal and target towing for the UK armed forces, as well as navigational aid calibration services and oil spill response aircraft.

In July 2019 the company was bought out by Advent who, despite assurances that national security wouldn't be affected, then sold the bulk of operations to overseas buyers eighteen months later. The company was split up into different arms and the hangars at Bournemouth Airport that were formerly Cobham Aviation Services became emblazoned with the name Draken, who purchased that arm of the business in 2020 and then subsequently became Draken Europe.

Meanwhile, Bournemouth International Airport had been bought by Bournemouth Corporation and Dorset County Council in 1969; then in 1978, Channel Express Air Services was established and operated daily services to the Channel Islands using Handley Page Dart Herald Aircraft.

Channel Express Air Services also operated a flourishing nightly cargo trade, particularly with the Channel Islands, which started in 1972, when Channel Island tomato and flower growers were desperate to salvage a large consignment of tomatoes that was stranded in Jersey during a lorry drivers strike on the British mainland. Channel Express also had a contract with the Post Office in the early 1980s, whereby mail was flown from the south of England to Liverpool and vice versa. This service operated until 2015.

In 1995, National Express purchased the airport, before selling it to Manchester Airports Group in 1999, who in turn sold it to Regional and City Airports, part of Rigby Group PLC, in 2017. Since then the airport has seen an increase in use by charter airlines such as Ryanair and easyJet and around 750,000 passengers are transported through the airport every year.

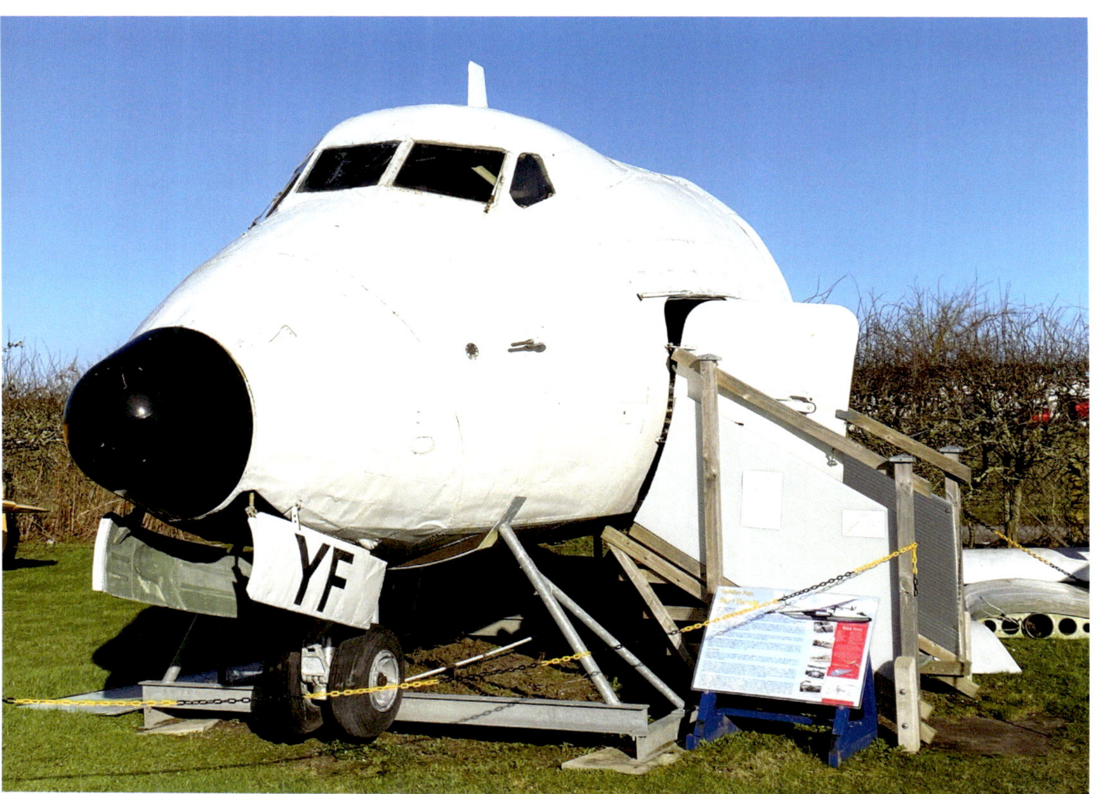

This is the nose section of the last ever Handley Page Herald to fly into Bournemouth Airport. She had been on the nightly Royal Mail return service to Liverpool on 9 April 1999. Bournemouth also witnessed the first flight of the Herald when a Jersey Airlines Herald landed in May 1961. (Published with the permission of Bournemouth Aviation Museum)

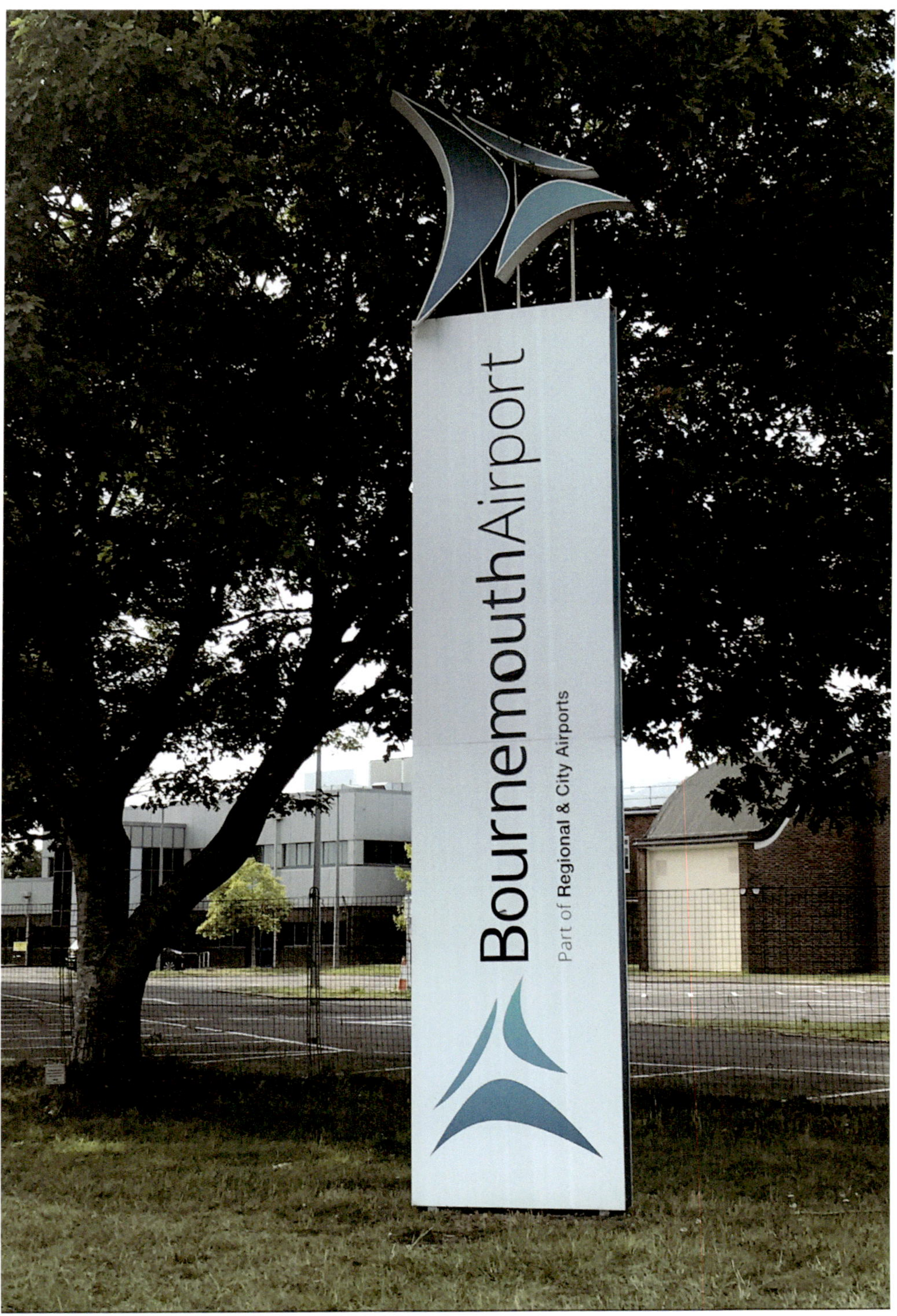

Bournemouth International Airport.

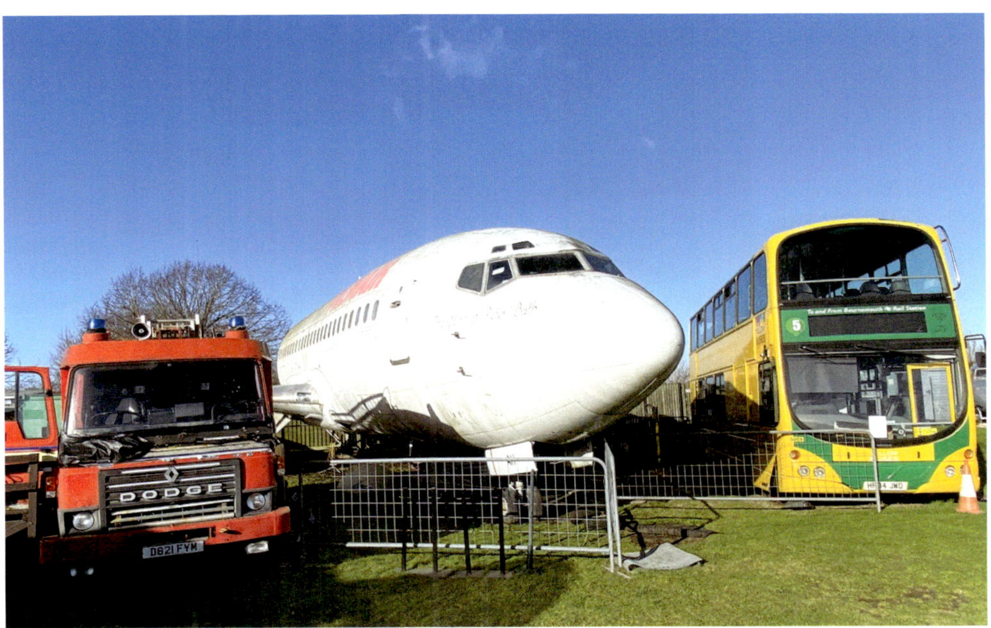

The Spirit of Peter Bath. The section of a Boeing 737 houses a tribute to Peter Bath, who was the gregarious managing director of Bath Travel and founder of Palmair. He was a pioneer of package holidays locally and made a point of personally greeting every passenger as they boarded the plane. (Published with the permission of Bournemouth Aviation Museum)

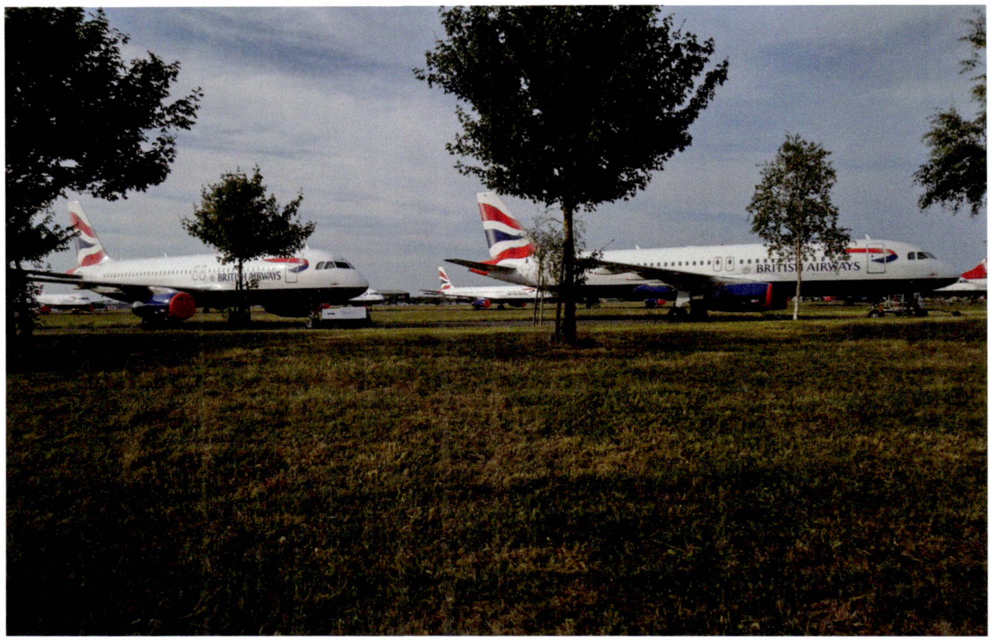

Grounded planes at Bournemouth Airport in 2020 due to the Covid-19 pandemic.

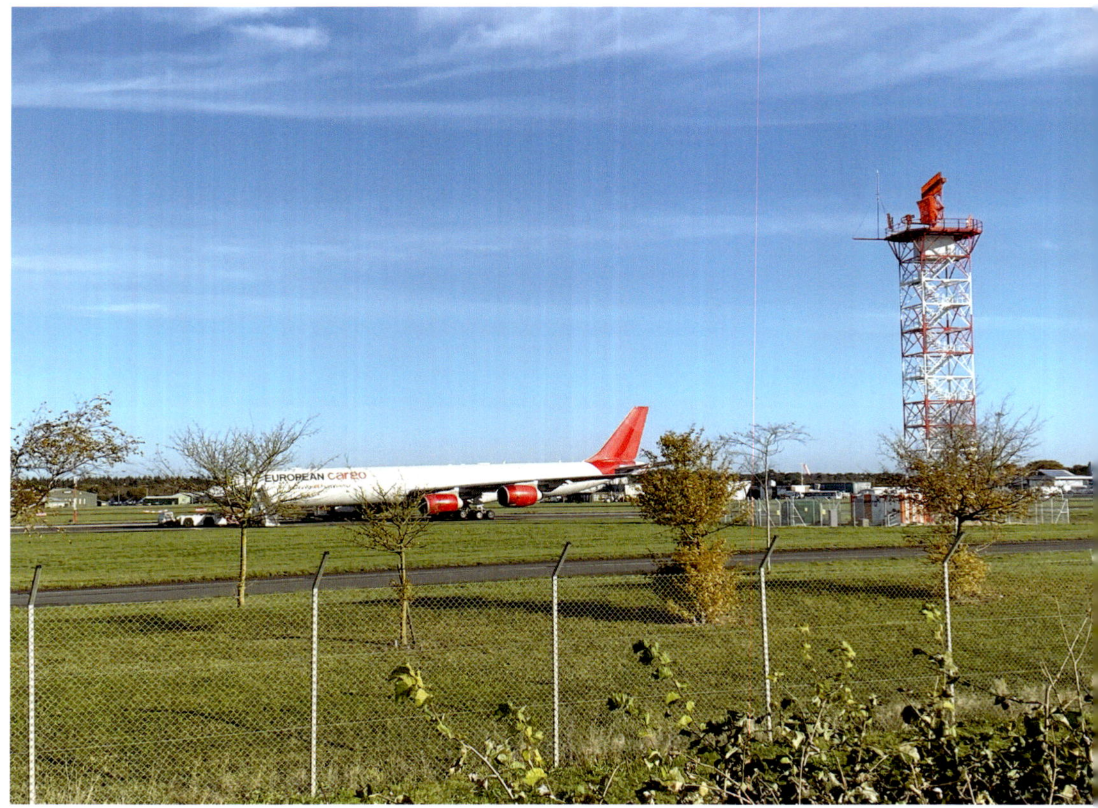

Bournemouth Airport in more conventional times.

From 1949 to 2011, Bournemouth Airport was also the home for the Ministry of Aviation School of Air Traffic Control. The college was based at what is now the Parkfield School complex and provided training for air traffic controllers and assistants for the United Kingdom as well as more than 140 other countries, before being relocated to Swanwick in Hampshire.

Bibliography

Ashley, H., *Bournemouth* (1988)

Did You Know? Bournemouth A Miscellany (Francis Frith, 2006)

Cullingford, C. N., A *History of Dorset* (Phillimore)

Draper, J., *Dorset: The Complete Guide* (Dovecote Press)

Flude, K., *Divorced, Beheaded, Died* (Michael O'Mara Books, 2015)

Hilliam, D., *The Little Book Of Dorset* (The History Press, 2010)

Jackson, A., *A-Z of Poole* (Amberley Publishing, 2020)

Jackson, A., *Once Upon a Time in the South West* (Amazon, 2021)

Jackson, A., *Poole Pubs* (Amberley Publishing, 2019)

Jackson, A., *Historic England: Dorset* (Amberley Publishing, 2020)

Jackson, A., *Secret Bournemouth* (Amberley Publishing, 2023)

Jackson, A., *Secret Swanage and Around* (Amberley Publishing, 2024)

Jackson, A., *The Jacobite Rebellions of the British Isles* (Pen and Sword Books, 2024)

Needham, J., *Bournemouth Past and Present* (The History Press, 2010)

Norman, A., *Founders and Famous Visitors* (The History Press, 2010)

Powell, S., *Bournemouth Aviation Museum Guide* (2023)

Perrin, L., *A Century of Bournemouth* (Sutton Publishers, 2002)

Richards, A., *Slow Travel Dorset* (Bradt, 2015)

Souden, D., *A Guide to Winchester Cathedral* (Winchester Cathedral. B.T. Basford Holdings Ltd, 2021)

Ward Lock and Co.'s *Bournemouth* (Ward Lock and Co.)

Leaflets

Destination Guide – Winchester – Winchester City Council

Royalists and Roundheads – Trail for Families – Winchester Cathedral

Anglo Saxon and Viking Trail – Winchester Cathedral

Display Aircraft – Tangmere Aviation Museum

The Great Hall of Fame – Hampshire County Council

The Great Hall – Where History and Legend Meet – Hampshire County Council

Additional Information From

Bournemouth Aviation Museum

Christchurch Ducking Stool

Christchurch Castle

Christchurch Priory

Hengistbury Head Visitor Centre

Old Custom House – Mudeford Quay – Information Board

Red House Museum
Tangmere Military Aviation Museum
Winchester Cathedral

Pubs
Ye Olde George Inne
The Haven House Inn
The Thomas Tripp
The Ship
The Ship in Distress

Websites
Aerosociety.com – Aeronautical Society – Dorset Aviation Past and Present
Baesystems.com – Airspeed Ambassador
Baesystems.com – Airspeed Horsa Glider
Baesystems.com – Vickers Varsity
Bournemouthecho.co.uk – 2 Cot 2017 – World War Two landmines could be buried under the zig zag paths
Britannica.com – Mosquito / Range, Top Speed, Variants and Specifications
Brooklandsmuseum.com – Vickers 668 Varsity T1
Dorsetcouncil.gov.uk
Dorsetlife.co.uk – The Bailey Bridge – published June 16
Dorsetlife.co.uk – Christchurch Castle and Hall – published October 14
H2g2.com – Christchurch Castle, Dorset, UK
Hampshireairfields.co.uk
Historychristchurch.org.uk
Newforestguide.uk
nfhwa.org – The Day a Luftwaffe plane landed at RAF Christchurch
rafmuseum.org
simpleflying.com – The Story of the Airspeed AS Ambassador
smuggling.co.uk – Smuggling in Hampshire